ck

BUGS

WITHDRAWN

FACTS AT YOUR FINGERTIPS

LONDON, NEW YORK, MUNICH,
MELBOURNE, and DELHI

DK DELHI
Project editor Pallavi Singh
Project art editor Deep Shikha Walia
Senior editor Kingshuk Ghoshal
Senior art editor Rajnish Kashyap
Editor Esha Banerjee
Assistant art editor Dhirendra Singh
DTP designers Neeraj Bhatia, Vishal Bhatia
Picture researcher Sumedha Chopra
Managing editor Saloni Talwar
Managing art editor Romi Chakraborty
CTS manager Balwant Singh
Production manager Pankaj Sharma

DK LONDON
Senior editor Fleur Star
Senior art editor Philip Letsu
US editor Margaret Parrish
Jacket editor Manisha Majithia
Jacket designer Laura Brim
Jacket manager Amanda Lunn
Production editor Adam Stoneham
Production controller Mary Slater

Publisher Andrew Macintyre
Associate publishing director Liz Wheeler
Art director Phil Ormerod
Publishing director Jonathan Metcalf

Consultant Richard Jones

TALL TREE LTD.
Editors Rob Colson, Joe Fullman, Jon Richards
Designer Ed Simkins

First published in the United States in 2012
by DK Publishing
375 Hudson Street, New York, New York 10014

Copyright © 2012 Dorling Kindersley Limited
12 13 14 15 16 10 9 8 7 6 5 4 3 2 1
001–184268–Nov/12

A catalog record for this book
is available from the Library of Congress.
ISBN: 978-0-7566-9814-0

Printed and bound by South China
Printing Company, China

Discover more at
www.dk.com

CONTENTS

 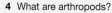
Scales and sizes
The book contains profiles of animals with scale drawings to show their size.

6 in (15 cm)

1½ in (4 cm)

Ants

What are arthropods?

Insects are arthropods, which are a type of invertebrate (animal without a backbone). Most of the arthropods on Earth are insects and they can be found almost all over the planet. Arthropods live in most habitats on land as well as in water. This book explores the world of land-based arthropods, many of which are commonly known as "bugs."

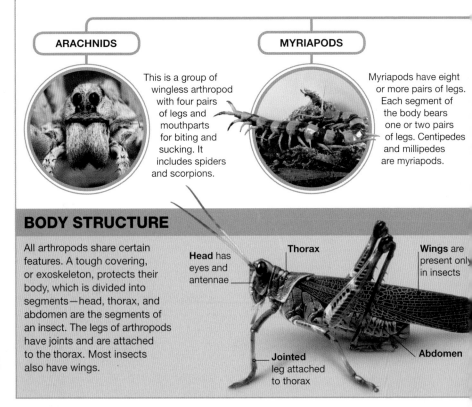

ARACHNIDS

This is a group of wingless arthropod with four pairs of legs and mouthparts for biting and sucking. It includes spiders and scorpions.

MYRIAPODS

Myriapods have eight or more pairs of legs. Each segment of the body bears one or two pairs of legs. Centipedes and millipedes are myriapods.

BODY STRUCTURE

All arthropods share certain features. A tough covering, or exoskeleton, protects their body, which is divided into segments—head, thorax, and abdomen are the segments of an insect. The legs of arthropods have joints and are attached to the thorax. Most insects also have wings.

Head has eyes and antennae

Thorax

Wings are present only in insects

Jointed leg attached to thorax

Abdomen

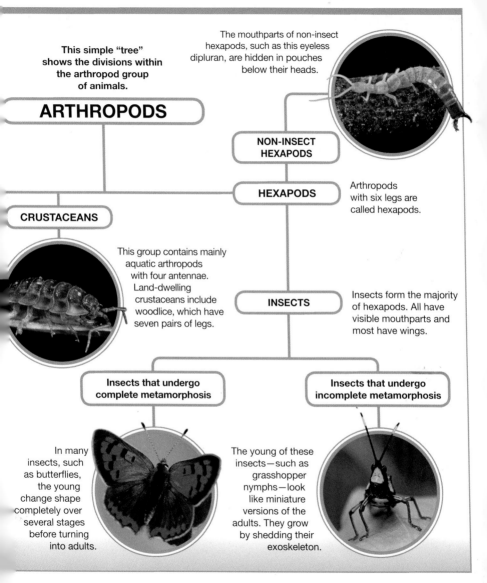

This simple "tree" shows the divisions within the arthropod group of animals.

The mouthparts of non-insect hexapods, such as this eyeless dipluran, are hidden in pouches below their heads.

ARTHROPODS

NON-INSECT HEXAPODS

HEXAPODS

Arthropods with six legs are called hexapods.

CRUSTACEANS

This group contains mainly aquatic arthropods with four antennae. Land-dwelling crustaceans include woodlice, which have seven pairs of legs.

INSECTS

Insects form the majority of hexapods. All have visible mouthparts and most have wings.

Insects that undergo complete metamorphosis

In many insects, such as butterflies, the young change shape completely over several stages before turning into adults.

Insects that undergo incomplete metamorphosis

The young of these insects—such as grasshopper nymphs—look like miniature versions of the adults. They grow by shedding their exoskeleton.

What is not an arthropod?

Tentacle

Many of the creepy crawlies you might think of as bugs are not true insects. Some are not even arthropods, but are different kinds of invertebrates—ranging from unmoving anemones on the ocean floor to worms wriggling through rainforests.

Muscular foot

Mollusks

This invertebrate group includes snails, mussels, and squid. Many mollusks use their flat, muscular feet to move. Some mollusks have calcium-rich shells covering their bodies, which protect them from predators.

Shell

A snail is a shelled mollusk

Cnidarians

The aquatic animals that make up this group of invertebrates have tubelike bodies with an opening at one end. Some cnidarians, such as jellyfish, float freely, while others, such as anemones, are attached to the ocean floor or to rocks under water. Sea anemones feed using their tentacles, which are lined with special structures that sting passing prey.

Worms

These soft-bodied, fleshy invertebrates lack an exoskeleton and do not have jointed legs. The green paddle worm has flaplike extensions that help it to slither around rocks as well as to swim in water.

Flaplike extensions on the body help the worm to move

Green paddle worm

Echinoderms

Echinoderms are sea-dwelling creatures that lack a well-defined head or tail. They have spiny bodies with a range of shapes—feathery, cylindrical, or with many arms. Sea cucumbers have cylindrical bodies and feed using their tentacle-shaped feet. The feet grab floating algae and tiny food particles from the ocean floor and put them in the organism's mouth.

Red-lined sea cucumber

Life cycle

Arthropods begin life as eggs. After the young hatch, they grow by shedding their exoskeleton at regular intervals. This is called molting. Myriapods and arachnids molt all their lives. Insects go through several stages of growth in a process called metamorphosis before turning into adults. Most adult arthropods reproduce by mating.

Mature adult has a bright red exoskeleton with black spots

Young adult emerges from pupa

Larva stops feeding and attaches itself to a leaf. Its outer skin hardens, and inside it begins to change into an adult. This stage of growth is called a **pupa**.

Complete metamorphosis

Insects such as wasps, butterflies, flies, and beetles go through complete metamorphosis. In these insects, the young, or larvae, look nothing like the adults they will become. The larvae change into adults over several stages of growth.

Larva molts several times and keeps renewing its exoskeleton as it grows

Incomplete metamorphosis

Insects such as grasshoppers and damselflies go through incomplete metamorphosis. Their young, or nymphs, look like smaller, wingless versions of adults. The nymphs molt several times and gradually turn into adults.

Azure damselfly lays **eggs** in pairs on the stems of aquatic plants

Egg hatches into a **nymph**, which lives underwater and molts several times

Nymph climbs out of water before its final molt and, later, a young adult emerges from the skin of the nymph

Newly formed wings are not yet ready for flight

Mature adult has fully developed wings and a bright green body

Adult seven-spot ladybugs mate to reproduce

Eggs laid on a leaf

Larva hatches from an egg

Asexual reproduction

In some arthropods, the females give birth without mating with a male. Females may also lay unfertilized eggs. These hatch into tiny young that look just like their mother, as in the case of this cottony cushion scale insect.

Feeding habits

Arthropods eat a wide range of food—dung, blood, plants, other arthropods, and even their own kind. Many arthropods have mouthparts that help them to feed on particular kinds of food. Butterflies, for example, have straw-shaped mouthparts that suck nectar from flowers.

Plant-eaters

Many arthropods feed on parts of plants, including fruits, leaves and sap. The larvae of moths and butterflies—called caterpillars—eat leaves using their mandibles (jaws).

Hunters

Predatory arthropods hunt other arthropods, and some can even kill small mammals, such as rats. Spiders are good predators, but can fall prey to the spider-hunting wasp, which paralyzes the spiders with its venom.

Spider-hunting wasp

Feeding on wood

Wood-eating arthropods range from pests that feed on trees to those that eat rotting wood. These species, such as woodlice, grow slowly because wood is not as nutritious as other kinds of food.

Woodlice feed on rotting wood

Eating dung

Some beetles breed in the dung of other animals. Dung beetles roll cattle dung into balls and lay eggs in it; the dung provides food for their larvae when they hatch.

Recycling dead remains

Many arthropods are scavengers and feed on decaying organic matter—the remains of dead plants and animals. Many lay eggs on the remains to provide food for their larvae. Sexton beetles, for example, bury carcasses (bodies of dead animals) in soil to feed their larvae.

PARASITISM

Abdomen of castor bean tick is swollen with host blood

Parasites
A parasite attaches itself to a larger animal—called a host—and feeds on the host's blood, before falling off. It does not kill the host.

Parasitoids
Braconid wasp larvae are parasitoids—they grow by feeding on a living host, such as a caterpillar, and then kill the host.

Habitats

The environment in which an organism lives is called its habitat. Arthropods are found in all kinds of habitat on land, including extreme places such as dry deserts and freezing polar regions.

In Alaska and other **snowy region** in the northern hemisphere, where temperatures are low and there is almost no vegetation, winter gnats survive even when there is snow on the ground.

North America

South America

Urban habitats

Some arthropods have adapted to life in human settlements, which are also called urban habitats. For example, cockroaches are often found crawling around houses in search of bits of food.

Grasslands support many arthropods, including dung beetles, which live among the tall grasses of these open areas and lay eggs in the dung of cattle.

The heat and humidity of **rainforests** help them to support the largest number of arthropods on Earth. This morpho butterfly is found in the rainforests of Ecuador.

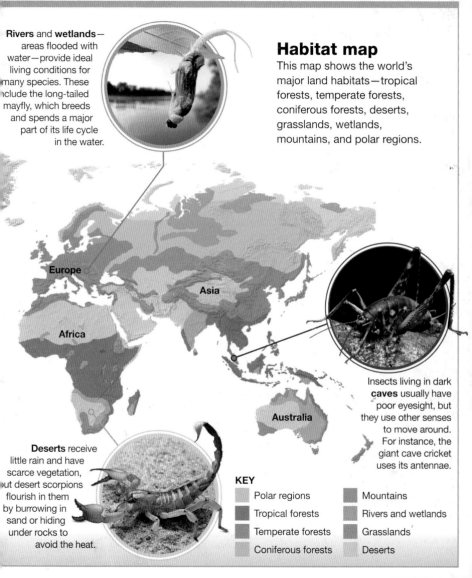

Rivers and wetlands— areas flooded with water—provide ideal living conditions for many species. These include the long-tailed mayfly, which breeds and spends a major part of its life cycle in the water.

Habitat map

This map shows the world's major land habitats—tropical forests, temperate forests, coniferous forests, deserts, grasslands, wetlands, mountains, and polar regions.

Europe

Asia

Africa

Australia

Insects living in dark caves usually have poor eyesight, but they use other senses to move around. For instance, the giant cave cricket uses its antennae.

Deserts receive little rain and have scarce vegetation, but desert scorpions flourish in them by burrowing in sand or hiding under rocks to avoid the heat.

KEY

Polar regions

Tropical forests

Temperate forests

Coniferous forests

Mountains

Rivers and wetlands

Grasslands

Deserts

Studying bugs

One of the best ways to learn about bugs is to study them close up, either by observing them in their natural habitats or by capturing one for a short time to study it even more closely. When studying bugs, it is important to keep a record of where a bug was found, as well as its appearance, behavior, and habitat.

Study kit

People often catch bugs using nets and trays. They then use a set of simple tools to study them, including pooters, tweezers, and brushes. Bugs are often released unharmed after observations are made.

Tweezers with fine tips for holding a bug

Brush for picking up and moving small insects

Fishing net collects bugs from ponds

Tray for holding bugs collected from ponds and rivers

Reading the signs

Sometimes, it is difficult to spot certain types of bug. However, it is possible to tell whether the bugs have visited a place recently by identifying the typical feeding and nesting signs they leave behind.

Gall wasps produce **swellings called galls** on oak leaves

Leaf beetle larvae produce these **patterns** when eating leaves

Froghopper nymphs produce **protective coverings** that look like froth

Web shapes can be used to identify types of spider

Intake tube to suck in air

Gauze

Homemade **pooter**—made from tubes and a glass jar—helps to suck up and hold small bugs. A piece of gauze tied to the end of the intake tube prevents bugs from being sucked into it.

Insect is sucked into longer tube

A **notebook** is a great way to quickly record a new observation. It can be used to draw a bug and record its features.

ARMY ANTS

These ants are a good example of insects that live and work together. At dawn, army ants emerge in their millions and march noisily along the forest floor in South America. Worker ants hold on to each other, forming "ant bridges," which allow other members of the colony to move quickly across cracks and streams.

A swarm of army ants can kill

100,000

insects, spiders, and even small mammals in a day

Insects

Insects make up nearly three-quarters of all animal species on Earth. They are small in size, breed rapidly, and flourish in almost all habitats on land—from mountains to seashores—as well as in fresh water and even on the ocean surface. Robber flies (left) are found worldwide, and they are among the many insects that can fly. Winged insects were the first animals to evolve powered flight, around 350 million years ago.

REPRODUCTION
Some insects, such as aphids, can reproduce without mating. An adult female produces many offspring that are identical to it.

What is an insect?

Like all arthropods, insects have jointed legs and a hard exoskeleton. The bodies of insects are divided into three sections—the head, thorax and abdomen. All insects have six legs, and most also have wings. Winged insects are the only arthropods that can fly.

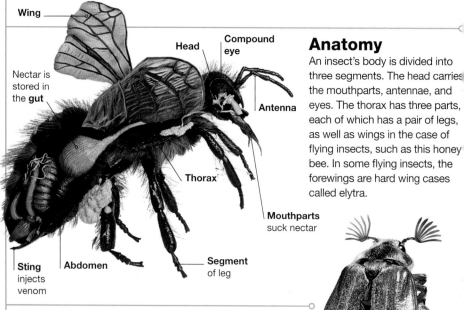

Wing

Nectar is stored in the **gut**

Head

Compound eye

Antenna

Thorax

Mouthparts suck nectar

Sting injects venom

Abdomen

Segment of leg

Anatomy

An insect's body is divided into three segments. The head carries the mouthparts, antennae, and eyes. The thorax has three parts, each of which has a pair of legs, as well as wings in the case of flying insects, such as this honey bee. In some flying insects, the forewings are hard wing cases called elytra.

Flight

Insects were the first animals to evolve powered flight, which allows them to look for food and escape quickly from danger. Most flying insects have two pairs of wings and can fold their wings when at rest.

1. Preparing to fly
As the cockchafer beetle prepares to fly, its elytra begin to open. It then uses its hind wings to fly.

Elytra protect sof hind wings

Why are insects widespread?

Insects have been around for about 400 million years and are widespread. They breed rapidly and flourish in most habitats on Earth, filling the tiniest spaces in a habitat because of their small size. A tough exoskeleton protects insects from predators and keeps them moist, letting them live in dry areas. The ability of most insects to fly allows them to find new habitats and sources of food.

Millions of termites live together in a single mound

Antennae spread out like a fan and check wind direction

Elytra do not flap in flight

Hind wings beat rapidly

Large, delicate **hind wing**

3. In flight
The beetle holds its legs outstretched, ready to catch hold of a surface on landing. The hind wings beat continuously to push the insect forward and steer it through the air.

2. Taking off
As the elytra open up, joints in the hind wings unfold, and they spread out fully. In flight, the open elytra provide a lifting force, just like the wings of an airplane.

Silverfish and bristletails

These wingless insects have a scaly body with three tails. Silverfish and firebrats make up the order Zygentoma, while bristletails form the order Archaeognatha.

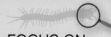
Common silverfish
Lepisma saccharina

Silverfish have three tails of the same length

The common silverfish can be spotted moving around at night in damp places, such as kitchens and bathrooms. Its body is covered in silver scales and tapers at the end, making it look like a fish. It also seems to wiggle like a fish while moving.

SIZE ½ in (1.2 cm) long

DIET Decaying organic matter and materials rich in sugar

HABITAT Caves, houses, and buildings

DISTRIBUTION Worldwide except polar regions

Firebrat
Thermobia domestica

Female firebrats can lay eggs only at temperatures between 90°F (32°C) and 106°F (41°C). For this reason, they are found in warm places, such as bakeries, as well as near ovens, fireplaces, boilers, and furnaces.

SIZE ½ in (1–1.5 cm) long

DIET Materials rich in sugar and proteins

HABITAT Rocky areas, leaf litter, houses, and buildings

DISTRIBUTION Worldwide except polar regions

Scales similar to those on silverfish

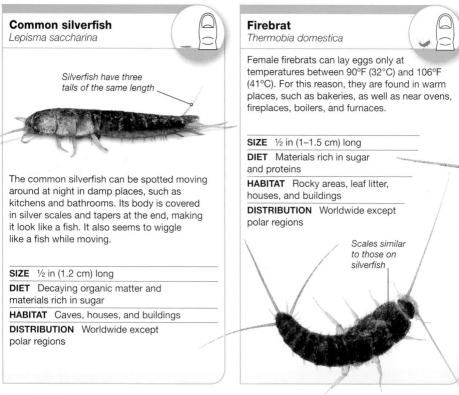

▲ Silverfish can be found feeding on egg cartons, which contain starch.

▲ Silverfish tend to damage books, feeding on the starch-rich paper.

Jumping bristletail
Petrobius maritimus

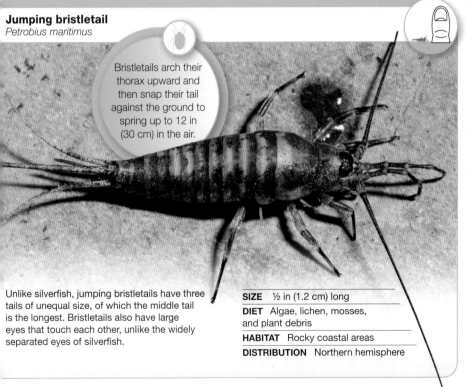

Bristletails arch their thorax upward and then snap their tail against the ground to spring up to 12 in (30 cm) in the air.

Unlike silverfish, jumping bristletails have three tails of unequal size, of which the middle tail is the longest. Bristletails also have large eyes that touch each other, unlike the widely separated eyes of silverfish.

SIZE ½ in (1.2 cm) long

DIET Algae, lichen, mosses, and plant debris

HABITAT Rocky coastal areas

DISTRIBUTION Northern hemisphere

Mayflies

About 3,000 species of mayfly make up Ephemeroptera—an order of primitive winged insects. Mayflies spend most of their lives as aquatic nymphs—the underwater nymphs can live for 1–2 years. These turn into short-lived adults that often die within a day.

Blue-winged olive
Serratella ignita

Males of this species have specially shaped eyes. The upper part of the eye is enlarged so they can see clearly above them. This is useful in large mating swarms. When a female enters the swarm, a male spots her easily from below and grabs her, prior to mating.

Mayfly
Ephemera danica

The underwater nymphs of this species feed in the silt at the bottom of rivers and lakes. A 2011 study has shown that rising temperatures in parts of northern England have caused the nymphs to eat more and grow faster. They now molt into adults within a year, instead of the previous two-year period.

Long front legs held forward

Three tails of equal length

SIZE ¾–1 in (1.7–2.5 cm) long

DIET Nymphs feed on dead and living algae; adults do not feed

HABITAT In and on vegetation near freshwater bodies

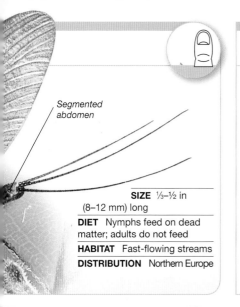

Segmented abdomen

SIZE ⅓–½ in (8–12 mm) long

DIET Nymphs feed on dead matter; adults do not feed

HABITAT Fast-flowing streams

DISTRIBUTION Northern Europe

Pond olive
Cloeon dipterum

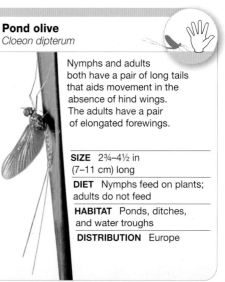

Nymphs and adults both have a pair of long tails that aids movement in the absence of hind wings. The adults have a pair of elongated forewings.

SIZE 2¾–4½ in (7–11 cm) long

DIET Nymphs feed on plants; adults do not feed

HABITAT Ponds, ditches, and water troughs

DISTRIBUTION Europe

Summer mayfly
Siphlonurus lacustris

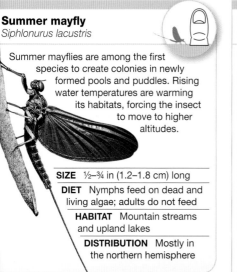

Summer mayflies are among the first species to create colonies in newly formed pools and puddles. Rising water temperatures are warming its habitats, forcing the insect to move to higher altitudes.

SIZE ½–¾ in (1.2–1.8 cm) long

DIET Nymphs feed on dead and living algae; adults do not feed

HABITAT Mountain streams and upland lakes

DISTRIBUTION Mostly in the northern hemisphere

Large dark olive
Baetis rhodani

This is one of the most widespread species of mayfly in Europe. Its cigar-shaped nymphs are active swimmers and can dart about quickly in water by flicking their abdomen and tails in an up and down motion.

SIZE ⅛–½ in (4–12 mm) long

DIET Nymphs feed on algae; adults do not feed

HABITAT Ditches, pools, and streams

DISTRIBUTION Europe

Damselflies and dragonflies

These fast-flying aerial hunters have long bodies and large eyes. There are about 5,600 species, and they make up the order Odonata.

Emerald damselfly
Lestes sponsa

The slim nymphs of this insect have a light green or brown body, and they mature into strong adults with a body that is brilliant metallic green. This damselfly is also known as spread-winged because, unlike most damselflies, it rests with its wings held out at an angle.

SIZE   1½ in (3.6 cm) long

DIET   Flies, mosquitoes, midges, and beetles

HABITAT   Slow-moving or still water in pools, lakes, streams, and canals

DISTRIBUTION   Europe and Asia

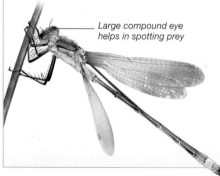

Large compound eye helps in spotting prey

Banded demoiselle
Calopteryx splendens

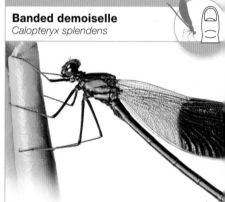

This species gets its name from the dark patches on the large wings of the male. An adult male uses claspers at the tip of its abdomen to hold a female during mating.

SIZE   1¾ in (4.6 cm) long

DIET   Nymphs feed on aquatic insects; adults do not feed

HABITAT   Swamps, ditches, pools, and slow-moving streams with muddy bottoms

DISTRIBUTION   Northern and western Europe

◀ A damselfly has a slender body with a broad head and eyes that are set apart from each other. When a damselfly rests, its wings are folded back against its body.

◀ A dragonfly has a stouter body and a narrower head, which is rounded, and has a pair of large eyes that touch each other. It rests with its wings open.

Azure damselfly
Coenagrion puella

Adult azure damselflies frequently mate and lay eggs. An adult male will grasp a female during mating and continues to do so during egg-laying. The female uses her ovipositor (egg-laying organ) first to slit the stems of aquatic plants and then lay pairs of eggs in the slits.

SIZE	1½ in (3.5) cm long
DIET	Nymphs feed on small aquatic animals; adults feed on small flying insects
HABITAT	Ponds, streams, and brackish water
DISTRIBUTION	Britain; central and southern Europe to Central Asia

Males have a blue or black abdomen

Prince baskettail
Epitheca princeps

Although this dragonfly can hunt near treetops, it usually flies near the water surface, where it patrols for prey. It spends most of its life airborne rather than at rest on plants.

Wing has a yellow tip

SIZE	3 in (8.5 cm) long
DIET	Mosquitoes
HABITAT	Ponds, lakes, creeks, and rivers
DISTRIBUTION	North America

Plains clubtail
Gomphus externus

Female has a striking black and yellow pattern on its body

Nymphs buried in mud under water breathe by pumping water in and out through the upturned, exposed tip of their abdomens.

Clubtails get their name from the clublike shape of their abdomen. The abdomen of the plains clubtail has a slight swelling just before the tip, which is more distinct in the females than in the males.

SIZE 2½ in (6 cm) long

DIET Nymphs feed on aquatic insects; adults feed on flying insects

HABITAT Near large, slow-moving, muddy streams and rivers

DISTRIBUTION US and Canada

Flame skimmer
Libellula saturata

Dragonflies of the genus *Libellula* are often called darters because they fly very quickly, changing direction rapidly. The dragonfly warns off its rivals by suddenly darting toward them from a resting position.

SIZE 3 in (7.6 cm) long

DIET Larvae feed on mosquito and mayfly larvae, freshwater shrimp, small fish, and tadpoles; adults feed on small flying insects, such as midges and mosquitoes

HABITAT Warm ponds, streams, and hot springs

DISTRIBUTION Southwestern US

Broad-bodied chaser
Libellula depressa

Adults can be seen flying over ponds and lakes in June and July to breed. Mature males are powder blue, while the females are brown. The females dip the tips of their abdomens in water to lay eggs.

SIZE 1½–1¾ in (4–4.5 cm) long

DIET Nymphs feed on aquatic insects; adults eat flying insects

HABITAT Forests and near slow-flowing streams and ponds

DISTRIBUTION Central Europe

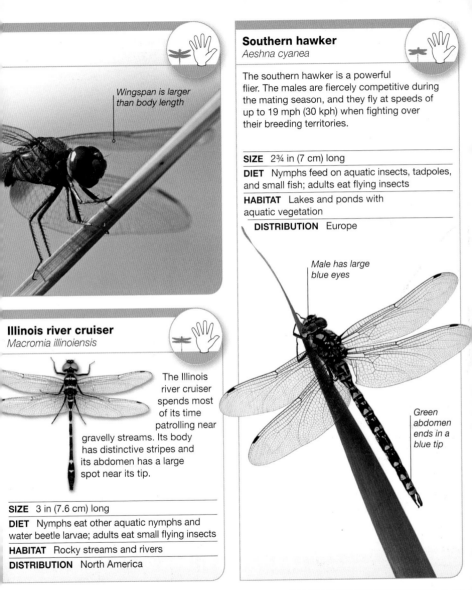

Wingspan is larger than body length

Illinois river cruiser
Macromia illinoiensis

The Illinois river cruiser spends most of its time patrolling near gravelly streams. Its body has distinctive stripes and its abdomen has a large spot near its tip.

SIZE 3 in (7.6 cm) long

DIET Nymphs eat other aquatic nymphs and water beetle larvae; adults eat small flying insects

HABITAT Rocky streams and rivers

DISTRIBUTION North America

Southern hawker
Aeshna cyanea

The southern hawker is a powerful flier. The males are fiercely competitive during the mating season, and they fly at speeds of up to 19 mph (30 kph) when fighting over their breeding territories.

SIZE 2¾ in (7 cm) long

DIET Nymphs feed on aquatic insects, tadpoles, and small fish; adults eat flying insects

HABITAT Lakes and ponds with aquatic vegetation

DISTRIBUTION Europe

Male has large blue eyes

Green abdomen ends in a blue tip

Stoneflies and rock crawlers

About 3,000 species of slim-bodied, winged insect called stoneflies make up the order Plecoptera. While the nymphs often feed on other insects, the adults do not eat and may only live for a day or two. The unrelated rock crawlers form the order Grylloblattodea. These tiny wingless bugs live in cold regions.

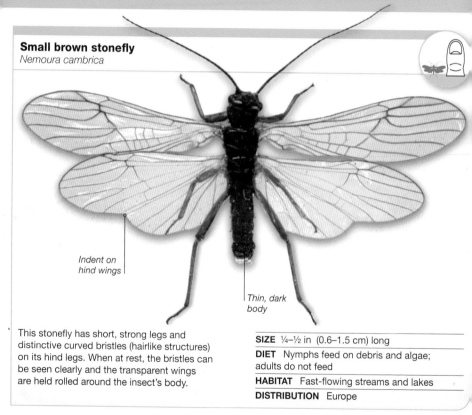

Small brown stonefly
Nemoura cambrica

Indent on
hind wings

Thin, dark
body

This stonefly has short, strong legs and distinctive curved bristles (hairlike structures) on its hind legs. When at rest, the bristles can be seen clearly and the transparent wings are held rolled around the insect's body.

SIZE ¼–½ in (0.6–1.5 cm) long

DIET Nymphs feed on debris and algae; adults do not feed

HABITAT Fast-flowing streams and lakes

DISTRIBUTION Europe

Pale stonefly
Perla bipunctata

Adult stoneflies are weak fliers and often rest on stones near the water's edge. The males of this species are about half the size of the females and have much shorter wings. The forewings of the females have ladderlike patterns made of numerous veins crossing each other.

Females have larger wings than males

SIZE ¾–1 in (2–2.8 cm) long

DIET Nymphs feed on caddisflies, larval mayflies, and non-biting midges; adults do not feed

HABITAT Stony streams in upland regions

DISTRIBUTION Europe and Africa

Yellow sally
Isoperla grammatica

Nymphs of this stonefly live under stones where predators, such as fish, cannot find them. Unlike in most other stoneflies, the nymphs of this species turn into winged adults during the day. Flying adults appear as a yellow blur in sunlight.

SIZE ⅓–½ in (0.9–1.3 cm) long

DIET Small insects and dead matter

HABITAT Gravel-bottomed streams and stony lakes

DISTRIBUTION Europe

Northern rock crawler
Grylloblatta campodeiformis

Cylindrical abdomen

This nocturnal insect is found on many mountains in North America. Its reproductive cycle is quite long—the female lays her eggs two months after mating, and the nymphs take about five years to mature.

SIZE ½–1¼ in (1.2–3 cm) long

DIET Dead insects, mosses, and plant matter

HABITAT Rocks near glaciers, limestone caves

DISTRIBUTION US and Canada

Stick and leaf insects

The order Phasmatodea is made up of about 3,000 species, which are usually active at night. These insects have evolved remarkable shapes resembling leaves and sticks, which help hide them in their forest habitats.

Macleay's spectre
Extatosoma tiaratum

Adult females of this species are wingless, as seen here, and are larger than the males. An adult female lays about a dozen eggs every day and scatters them around by flicking them away with her abdomen.

SIZE 1–11½ in (2.5–29 cm) long

DIET Leaves of eucalyptus trees

HABITAT Forests, grasslands, and rainforests

DISTRIBUTION Australia and New Guinea

Two-striped stick insect
Anisomorpha buprestoides

When threatened, this stick insect squirts a foul-smelling liquid from the front of its thorax. This liquid contains a chemical that irritates the eyes of the attacker.

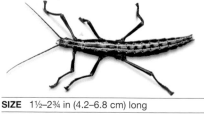

SIZE 1½–2¾ in (4.2–6.8 cm) long

DIET Leaves of shrubs and trees

HABITAT Tropical regions

DISTRIBUTION Southern US

Stick insect
Pharnacia sp.

These insects are known as walking sticks because of their extremely long and slender bodies. The female stick insect is wingless and can hold its legs close to its body, making it look even more like a twig.

SIZE 1–1¼ in (2.5–2.9 cm)

DIET Foliage

HABITAT Shrubs and trees

DISTRIBUTION India

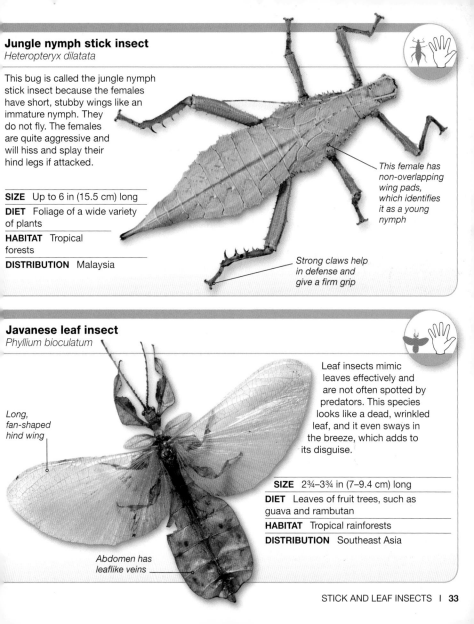

Jungle nymph stick insect
Heteropteryx dilatata

This bug is called the jungle nymph stick insect because the females have short, stubby wings like an immature nymph. They do not fly. The females are quite aggressive and will hiss and splay their hind legs if attacked.

SIZE Up to 6 in (15.5 cm) long

DIET Foliage of a wide variety of plants

HABITAT Tropical forests

DISTRIBUTION Malaysia

This female has non-overlapping wing pads, which identifies it as a young nymph

Strong claws help in defense and give a firm grip

Javanese leaf insect
Phyllium bioculatum

Leaf insects mimic leaves effectively and are not often spotted by predators. This species looks like a dead, wrinkled leaf, and it even sways in the breeze, which adds to its disguise.

Long, fan-shaped hind wing

SIZE 2¾–3¾ in (7–9.4 cm) long

DIET Leaves of fruit trees, such as guava and rambutan

HABITAT Tropical rainforests

DISTRIBUTION Southeast Asia

Abdomen has leaflike veins

WALKING LEAF
Adult females of this species have wider abdomens than the males. The abdomen has two pale spots that look like faded holes on a leaf, which adds to the insect's camouflage.

Walking leaf insects mimic their surroundings so well that other leaf insects often try to

take bites

out of them

Earwigs

There are about 1,900 species of earwig. These plant-eating and scavenging insects form the order Dermaptera. Most have short forewings and fanlike hind wings that can be folded. The abdomen ends in a pair of pincers, which are called forceps.

Two-spotted earwig
Anechura bipunctata

In many species of earwig, female parents often make good mothers. The females of this wingless species lay eggs in soil and take care of them until they hatch. They protect the eggs with their slender pincers and also feed the nymphs after they hatch.

Tawny earwig
Labidura riparia

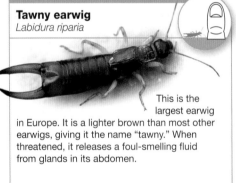

This is the largest earwig in Europe. It is a lighter brown than most other earwigs, giving it the name "tawny." When threatened, it releases a foul-smelling fluid from glands in its abdomen.

SIZE	¾ in (1.8 cm) long
DIET	Decaying matter
HABITAT	Sandy river banks and coastal areas
DISTRIBUTION	Worldwide except polar regions

Common earwig
Forficula auricularia

The forceps of this earwig are long and curved and have sharp structures on their inner sides. The earwig uses its forceps in defense and also to fold away its delicate hind wings, which are used in flight.

SIZE ½ in (1.4 cm) long

DIET Plants and decaying organic matter

HABITAT Woodlands and gardens

DISTRIBUTION Worldwide except polar regions

Lesser earwig
Labia minor

The lesser earwig is the smallest European earwig. It is a strong flier with fully developed wings that are reddish brown in color.

SIZE Less than ¼ in (7 mm) long

DIET Decaying plant material

HABITAT Compost heaps and rotting vegetation

DISTRIBUTION Europe

Females of this species take care of their eggs by licking dirt and fungal spores off them to keep them clean.

SIZE ½ in (1–1.5 cm) long

DIET Small insects, decaying plants, and animals

HABITAT Woodlands

DISTRIBUTION Europe

Mantises

The order Mantodea is made up of more than 2,300 species of mantis. They have triangular heads, large compound eyes, and flexible necks. Mantises are the only insects that can turn their heads around to look behind them.

FOCUS ON...
DEFENSE
Mantises defend themselves in many different ways.

Orchid mantis
Hymenopus coronatus

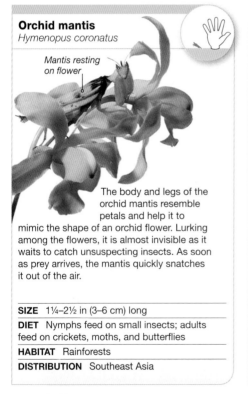

Mantis resting on flower

The body and legs of the orchid mantis resemble petals and help it to mimic the shape of an orchid flower. Lurking among the flowers, it is almost invisible as it waits to catch unsuspecting insects. As soon as prey arrives, the mantis quickly snatches it out of the air.

SIZE	1¼–2½ in (3–6 cm) long
DIET	Nymphs feed on small insects; adults feed on crickets, moths, and butterflies
HABITAT	Rainforests
DISTRIBUTION	Southeast Asia

Common praying mantis
Mantis religiosa

All mantises have the same resting pose—they hold their front legs up and together, as if in prayer. The forward-facing eyes of this species help the mantis to judge the distance to its prey accurately before it attacks.

Leaflike forewing

◀ The head, thorax, and abdomen of the leaf mantis mimic the appearance of a leaf. This helps to camouflage, or disguise, the insect.

◀ When threatened, the dead leaf mantis startles predators by raising its front legs and lifting its wings. This reveals bright markings on its underside.

Large compound eye

Spiny forelegs help to attack and hold prey

SIZE 2–3 in (5–7.4 cm) long

DIET Moths, crickets, grasshoppers, and flies

HABITAT Trees and shrubs

DISTRIBUTION Central and southern Europe

Conehead mantis
Empusa pennata

This species is easily identified by the distinctive crest on top of its head. The conehead mantis has a slim body, and parts of its abdomen have leaflike extensions, which help to camouflage the insect. Females have extremely thin antennae.

SIZE 2½ in (6 cm) long

DIET Small flies

HABITAT Grasslands and scrublands

DISTRIBUTION Southern Europe

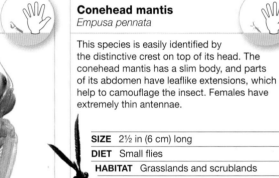

Small lobe on leg

Crickets and grasshoppers

Most crickets and grasshoppers have large wings, but instead of flying away when threatened, they tend to jump away using their powerful hind legs. Many adult males rub their legs or wings together and "sing" to attract mates. More than 25,000 species of these two groups of insect form the order Orthoptera.

Desert locust
Schistocerca gregaria

Desert locusts are grasshoppers that form swarms. After heavy rainfall, solitary locusts come together to feed. Crowding together stimulates them to release pheromones (scent chemicals) that cause the locusts to fly together in large swarms of up to 10 billion individuals, which can strip fields of crops within hours.

SIZE	Up to 3 in (7.5 cm) long
DIET	Grasses, crops, and other vegetation
HABITAT	Deserts, grasslands, and farmlands
DISTRIBUTION	North Africa and the Middle East

Strong hind legs aid in jumping

Mottled wings

House cricket
Acheta domestica

This cricket is only active at night. Males make chirping songs by rubbing their forewings against each other. Females are attracted to louder chirps, since they are usually made by larger males, which are more likely to produce strong, healthy offspring.

Dull brown coloration

SIZE	1 in (2.4 cm) long
DIET	Organic matter
HABITAT	Forests and grasslands
DISTRIBUTION	Southwestern Asia, Northern Africa, and Europe

Foaming grasshopper
Dictyophorus spumans

Vivid colors on the body of this grasshopper warn predators that it tastes foul. When threatened, it can also ward off predators by producing toxic foam from glands in its thorax.

Warty surface

SIZE	2½–3¼ in (6–8 cm) long
DIET	Milkweed
HABITAT	Rocky areas with low vegetation
DISTRIBUTION	South Africa

African cave cricket
Phaeophilacris geertsi

The African cave cricket is wingless and has long hind legs. This scavenger has very long antennae, which are useful in sensing its surroundings and predators in the darkness of the caves where it lives.

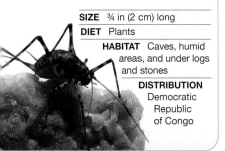

SIZE	¾ in (2 cm) long
DIET	Plants
HABITAT	Caves, humid areas, and under logs and stones
DISTRIBUTION	Democratic Republic of Congo

Mole cricket
Gryllotalpa gryllotalpa

Like a miniature mole, this insect uses its strong forelegs to dig burrows in soil for shelter. It uses its hind legs for pushing soil away while it digs. Mole crickets feed underground in the day and on the surface at night.

SIZE	1½–1¾ in (4–4.5 cm) long
DIET	Plant roots and invertebrates
HABITAT	Meadows and river banks
DISTRIBUTION	Europe

Cockroaches

These scavenging insects have flat, oval bodies that enable them to squeeze through tight spaces. Their sensitivity to vibrations allows them to detect predators early and so evade them. Around 4,600 species of cockroach make up the order Blattodea.

FOCUS ON...
HABITATS

Cockroaches have adapted to survive in a wide range of habitats.

▲ The American cockroach lurks around in houses, usually where there is a lot of food.

▲ Cockroaches of the *Desmozosteria* genus are fast-running daytime species found in deserts in western Australia.

▲ *Gyna laticosta* is a species that lives on the floor of a rainforest in Cameroon. It is disguised as a yellow leaf.

Long-winged great cockroach
Megaloblatta longipennis

This insect is the largest winged cockroach in the world and has a wingspan of 8 in (20 cm). Females tend to be very fertile, breeding five to six times a year. They produce about 40 eggs each time and about a thousand eggs in a lifetime.

Thin, long antenna

SIZE 2½ in (6 cm) long

DIET Plant materials

HABITAT Woodland litter, debris, and buildings

DISTRIBUTION Peru, Ecuador, and Panama

Dusky cockroach
Ectobius lapponicus

Dusky cockroaches run very fast. The males and females are active at different times of the day—the males in the afternoon and the females after sunset.

SIZE ⅓–½ in (0.8–1.3 cm) long

DIET Decaying organic matter

HABITAT Leaf litter and foliage

DISTRIBUTION Europe; introduced to US

American cockroach
Periplaneta americana

Originally from Africa, this species has spread worldwide by stowing away on ships. The cockroach's antennae are almost as long as its body.

SIZE 1¾ in (4.4 cm) long

DIET Decaying organic matter; stored or spilled food

HABITAT Houses, stores, and food warehouses

DISTRIBUTION Worldwide except in polar regions

Madagascan hissing cockroach
Gromphadorhina portentosa

Unlike most cockroaches, the Madagascan hissing cockroach is wingless. True to its name, it startles predators by squeezing air out of its spiracles (respiratory openings on the body of an insect), which produces a loud hiss.

Males use the "humps" on their thorax to engage in combat with rival males.

"Hump"

Spiracle

SIZE 2½–3¼ in (6–8 cm) long

DIET Dung

HABITAT Tropical regions

DISTRIBUTION Central America

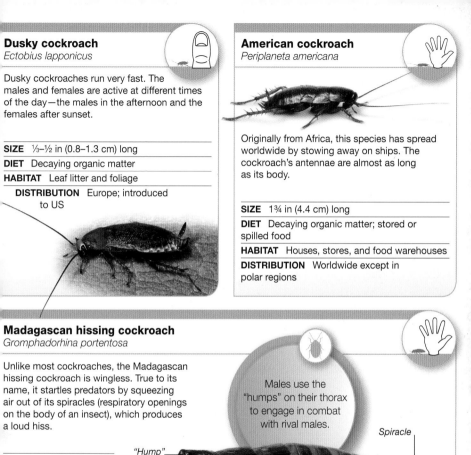

Termites and thrips

Termites are social insects that live in colonies, which may include more than a million termites. About 2,900 species of termite form the order Isoptera. The 7,400 species of thrip make up the order Thysanoptera. These tiny insects have two pairs of narrow wings lined with hair.

Formosan termite
Coptotermes formosanus

These termites forage for food by tunneling through soil, traveling up to 300 ft (100 m) if needed. Large colonies made up of several million termites can feed on about 13 oz (400 g) of wood in one day. This can severely damage structures made of wood.

SIZE ¼ in (6–7 mm) long

DIET Wood and materials containing cellulose, such as paper and cardboard

HABITAT Tropical and subtropical regions

DISTRIBUTION China and Japan; introduced to US and South Africa

Harvester termite
Macrotermes sp.

Termites in the genus *Macrotermes* are the farmers of the insect world. They cultivate gardens of fungi inside their massive mounds. The fungi grows on chewed pieces of wood and plant matter brought back by the adult termites.

SIZE ⅛–½ in (4–14 mm) long

DIET Fungi grown in nest

HABITAT Tropical forests, rainforests, and grasslands

DISTRIBUTION Africa and Asia

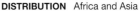

Pacific dampwood termite
Zootermopsis angusticollis

Unlike most termites that live on or near dry wood, this species needs wet conditions. It builds colonies in damp wood, such as rotting stumps and logs. About 4,000 termites make up a colony.

SIZE	1 in (2.4 cm) long
DIET	Damp, decaying wood
HABITAT	Humid, woody regions
DISTRIBUTION	Pacific coast of North America

Gladiolus thrip
Thrips simplex

The gladiolus thrip is found wherever gladiolus plants are grown. This insect uses its sucking mouthparts to feed on the plant sap, which deforms and discolors the flowers.

SIZE	Less than 1/16 in (2 mm) long
DIET	Plant sap
HABITAT	In leaf litter, and on leaves, flowers, and fruits of gladiolus plants
DISTRIBUTION	Africa, Asia, Europe, and North America

Flower thrip
Frankliniella sp.

Flattened body

Segmented antenna

A female flower thrip uses its sawlike ovipositor (egg-laying organ) to cut into a leaf, stem, or fruit of a plant before laying a single egg in each slit. The eggs stay protected within the plant. After hatching, the nymphs feed on the plant's juices.

SIZE	1/32–1/16 in (1–1.5 mm) long
DIET	Plant sap
HABITAT	Areas with vegetation and human settlements
DISTRIBUTION	Worldwide except polar regions

True bugs

This diverse group of insects is made up of 100,000 species, which include cicadas, hoppers, aphids, and water bugs. All the insects in this order—Hemiptera—have a beaklike mouthpart used for sucking plant sap, dissolved body tissues of prey, or blood.

Wart-headed bug
Phrictus quinquepartitus

A wart-headed bug has colorful hind wings. Their bright, flashy colors startle or confuse approaching predators. A greenish-yellow pattern on the forewings helps this bug to blend in well with its leafy surroundings.

Distinctive pattern on forewing

SIZE 2¼ in (5.5 cm) long

DIET Plant sap

HABITAT
Woodlands and forests

DISTRIBUTION
Costa Rica, Panama, Colombia, and parts of Brazil

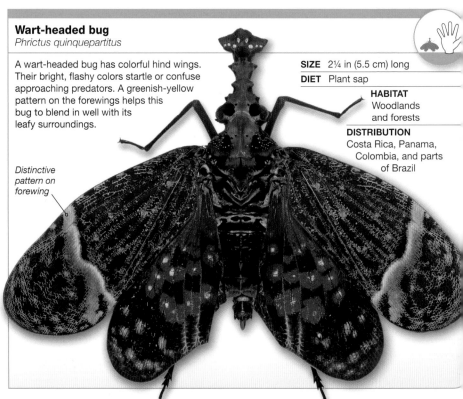

Indian cicada
Angamiana aetherea

Cicadas are noisy creatures. The male Indian cicada sings loudly to attract females as well as to deter rivals. It does this by rapidly vibrating a pair of drumlike organs on the side of its abdomen to produce a series of loud clicks.

SIZE 1½ in (3.5–4 cm) long

DIET Plants and roots

HABITAT Trees and shrubs in warm regions

DISTRIBUTION India

Froghopper
Cecopis vulnerata

These brightly colored bugs have strong legs that help to make them good jumpers. The females lay eggs in soil or on plants. Once hatched, the nymphs produce a foamlike substance that covers them in a protective layer and keeps them moist.

SIZE ½ in (1–1.2 cm) long

DIET Plant root sap

HABITAT Grassy areas and meadows

DISTRIBUTION Europe and Asia

Thorn bug
Umbonia crassicornis

The upper part of this insect's body has a sharp, pointed shape, which protects the slender bug by camouflaging it. To a predator, this bug looks like a thorn on a plant.

Pronotum (upper surface of thorax)

SIZE ½ in (1–1.2 cm) long

DIET Plant sap

HABITAT Woodlands and forests

DISTRIBUTION North and South America, and Southeast Asia

American lupin aphid
Macrosiphum albifrons

Thousands of aphids are often seen sucking on a single plant. Female aphids can produce hundreds of young without mating. The high rate of reproduction of aphids makes these plant eaters very destructive to crops.

SIZE ¼ in (5 mm) long

DIET Plants

HABITAT Wild and cultivated plants in northern temperate regions

DISTRIBUTION North America and Europe

Giant water bug
Lethocerus grandis

Hairs on hind legs aid in swimming

Pair of appendages used to breathe underwater

Pear psylla
Cacopsylla pyricola

The pear psylla is a pest of pear trees. The females lay eggs on, or in, these plants. Both the nymphs and the adults feed on the sap of the pear plants.

SIZE ¹⁄₁₆–¼ in (1.5–5 mm) long

DIET Plant sap

HABITAT Pear trees

DISTRIBUTION Europe, Asia, and US

Common pond skater
Gerris lacustris

The long legs of this insect spread its weight over the water surface, helping it to "walk" on water. It finds prey by using special sensitive hairs on its legs that detect ripples created by its victims.

SIZE ½ in (1–1.2 cm) long

DIET Other insects

HABITAT Ponds, streams, rivers, and lakes

DISTRIBUTION Worldwide except polar regions

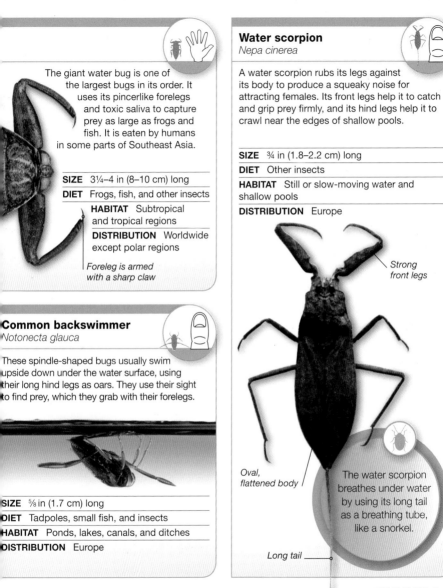

The giant water bug is one of the largest bugs in its order. It uses its pincerlike forelegs and toxic saliva to capture prey as large as frogs and fish. It is eaten by humans in some parts of Southeast Asia.

SIZE 3¼–4 in (8–10 cm) long

DIET Frogs, fish, and other insects

HABITAT Subtropical and tropical regions

DISTRIBUTION Worldwide except polar regions

Foreleg is armed with a sharp claw

Common backswimmer
Notonecta glauca

These spindle-shaped bugs usually swim upside down under the water surface, using their long hind legs as oars. They use their sight to find prey, which they grab with their forelegs.

SIZE ⅝ in (1.7 cm) long

DIET Tadpoles, small fish, and insects

HABITAT Ponds, lakes, canals, and ditches

DISTRIBUTION Europe

Water scorpion
Nepa cinerea

A water scorpion rubs its legs against its body to produce a squeaky noise for attracting females. Its front legs help it to catch and grip prey firmly, and its hind legs help it to crawl near the edges of shallow pools.

SIZE ¾ in (1.8–2.2 cm) long

DIET Other insects

HABITAT Still or slow-moving water and shallow pools

DISTRIBUTION Europe

Strong front legs

Oval, flattened body

The water scorpion breathes under water by using its long tail as a breathing tube, like a snorkel.

Long tail

Bed bug
Cimex lectularius

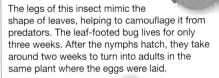

Bed bugs are parasites that feed on the blood of humans and other warm-blooded mammals. They feed only at night and go back into hiding during the day. This insect is wingless and has a flat body.

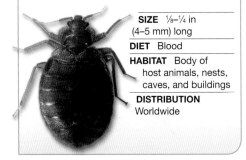

SIZE ⅛–¼ in (4–5 mm) long

DIET Blood

HABITAT Body of host animals, nests, caves, and buildings

DISTRIBUTION Worldwide

Common green capsid
Lygocoris pabulinus

Common green capsids belong to the largest family of true bugs. They are a serious pest of fruit crops, such as pears, apples, and raspberries. Raised, wartlike spots are left on fruits after this bug has finished feeding.

SIZE ¼ in (6 mm) long

DIET Sap of fruit and vegetable plants

HABITAT Areas with dense vegetation and field crops

DISTRIBUTION Europe

Leaf-footed bug
Bitta flavolineata

The legs of this insect mimic the shape of leaves, helping to camouflage it from predators. The leaf-footed bug lives for only three weeks. After the nymphs hatch, they take around two weeks to turn into adults in the same plant where the eggs were laid.

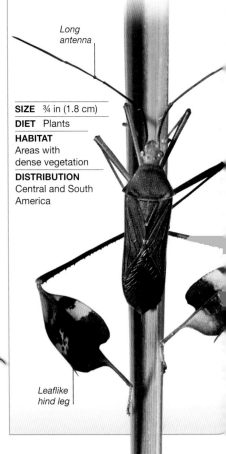

Long antenna

SIZE ¾ in (1.8 cm)

DIET Plants

HABITAT Areas with dense vegetation

DISTRIBUTION Central and South America

Leaflike hind leg

Scarlet shield bug
Eurydema dominulus

Bold colors on the body of this bug warn predators that it has a foul taste. Also known as the brassica bug, this insect is a serious pest of brassica plants, such as cabbage and turnips.

Red and black pronotum (upper part of thorax)

Large black patch on scutellum (triangular structure behind pronotum)

SIZE ⅓ in (8 mm) long

DIET Plants

HABITAT Woodlands and fields of cabbage and turnips

DISTRIBUTION Europe

White-spotted assassin bug
Platymeris biguttata

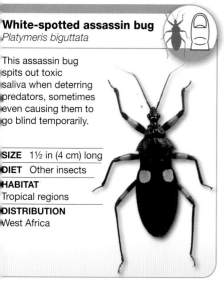

This assassin bug spits out toxic saliva when deterring predators, sometimes even causing them to go blind temporarily.

SIZE 1½ in (4 cm) long

DIET Other insects

HABITAT Tropical regions

DISTRIBUTION West Africa

Thistle lace bug
Tingis cardui

The fine pattern on the wings and upper body of this small insect give it a lacelike appearance. Its body is covered in powdery wax, which makes it look pale gray.

SIZE ⅛–³⁄₁₆ in (3–4 mm) long

DIET Spear, musk, and marsh thistles

HABITAT Grasslands

DISTRIBUTION Western Europe

SCARLET SHIELD BUG

True to their name, the creatures of the shield bug family have a tough exoskeleton that looks a bit like a shield. Their leathery forewings and thin hind wings are not very flexible and rattle when beating together in flight.

Some Mexican salsas have a special ingredient— scarlet shield bugs

Lice

The 5,200 species of louse in the order Phthiraptera are wingless and live on birds and mammals as parasites, using sucking mouthparts to feed on their blood. The related barklice and booklice are scavengers that belong to the order Psocoptera and number around 5,600 species.

Human head louse
Pediculus humanus capitis

The human head louse spends its life on the human scalp. An adult female lays about 9–10 eggs a day and attaches each egg separately to a strand of hair using a gluelike secretion. Once in place, the eggs are difficult to remove.

Claw grips tightly to hair shaft

Flat, pear-shaped body

SIZE ¹⁄₁₆–¹⁄₈ in (2–3 mm) long

DIET Blood

HABITAT On humans

DISTRIBUTION Worldwide except polar regions

Chicken body louse
Menacanthus stramineus

This insect can cause feather loss and infection in poultry. It lives near the base of the feathers on the body of the birds and holds on tightly with the claws on its strong legs.

SIZE ¼ in (5 mm) long

DIET Feather fragments, blood, and skin secretions

HABITAT On poultry

DISTRIBUTION Worldwide except polar regions

Goat louse
Damalinia limbata

The goat louse infests goats and sheep. It feeds on fat secretions on the skin of the host mammal. It also causes irritation on the skin of these animals and even damages wool in sheep. A single infected goat or sheep can spread the lice to an entire herd.

SIZE $\frac{1}{32}$–$\frac{1}{16}$ in (1–2 mm) long

DIET Skin, hair, secretions, and blood

HABITAT On goats and sheep

DISTRIBUTION Worldwide except polar regions

Flour louse
Liposcelis liparius

Needing high levels of moisture to survive, flour lice live in damp areas. If conditions get very damp, they multiply and become pests, damaging stored grain and books.

SIZE $\frac{5}{8}$ in (1.5 mm) long

DIET Fungi and decaying organic matter

HABITAT Damp and dark areas in human settlements

DISTRIBUTION Worldwide except polar regions

Bark louse
Psococerastis gibbosa

Unlike parasitic lice, the bark louse has wings, which are held rooflike over its body while it rests. This insect is commonly seen resting on trees and lays its eggs in the bark.

SIZE $\frac{1}{4}$ in (6 mm) long

DIET Fungi, decaying organic matter, pollen, and algae

HABITAT On deciduous and coniferous trees

DISTRIBUTION Europe and Asia

Large, bulging eyes

FOCUS ON...
OCELLI

Many arthropods have ocelli, or simple eyes, in addition to their compound eyes. The ocelli only sense light.

▲ Dobsonflies have three ocelli, arranged in a triangle on the head. These detect the horizon, allowing the insects to fly level.

▲ Alderflies lack ocelli and so are unsteady fliers.

Alderflies and relatives

The 300 species of alderfly and the related dobsonfly are weak fliers. They make up the order Megaloptera. Their aquatic larvae are predatory, while the adults do not feed.

Eastern dobsonfly
Corydalus cornutus

The males of this species have long, weak mandibles (jaws), which they use to grip the females during mating. The females have short, powerful mandibles and can deliver a painful bite if disturbed or threatened.

Wings are held like a roof over the body when at rest

SIZE	4 in (10 cm) long
DIET	Larvae feed on small aquatic insects and worms; adults do not feed
HABITAT	Streams, especially in temperate regions
DISTRIBUTION	North America

Fish fly
Chauliodes sp.

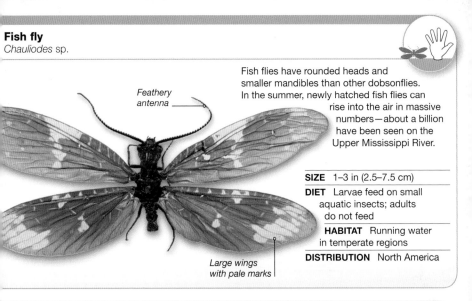

Fish flies have rounded heads and smaller mandibles than other dobsonflies. In the summer, newly hatched fish flies can rise into the air in massive numbers—about a billion have been seen on the Upper Mississippi River.

Feathery antenna

Large wings with pale marks

SIZE	1–3 in (2.5–7.5 cm)
DIET	Larvae feed on small aquatic insects; adults do not feed
HABITAT	Running water in temperate regions
DISTRIBUTION	North America

Alderfly
Sialis lutaria

Female alderflies can lay up to 2,000 eggs in a batch. The eggs are laid on twigs or leaves near water. The larvae drop into the water once they hatch. As they mature, they crawl out of the water and pupate in damp soil nearby, before turning into adults.

SIZE	½–¾ in (1.4–1.8 cm) long
DIET	Larvae feed on small aquatic insects and worms; adults do not feed
HABITAT	Muddy ponds, canals, and slow-moving water
DISTRIBUTION	Worldwide except polar regions

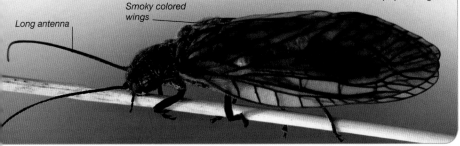

Smoky colored wings

Long antenna

Lacewings and relatives

The 7,000 species of lacewing and related bugs that make up the order Neuroptera have large eyes, chewing mouthparts, and long antennae. They all also hold their pairs of net-veined wings over their bodies when at rest.

Green lacewing
Chrysopa perla

Adult green lacewings can be identified by their blue-green body and the black veins on their wings. They are predators of aphids and lay eggs near aphid colonies. Their predatory larvae also feed on aphids.

SIZE	½ in (1–1.2 cm) long
DIET	Pollen, nectar, aphids, and honeydew
HABITAT	Deciduous woodlands
DISTRIBUTION	Europe

Veins arranged in a netlike pattern

Long antenna

Spoon-winged lacewing
Nemoptera sinuata

These insects are active only during the day. After hatching, the egg-shaped larvae stay hidden in sand and can detect the movement of prey by sensing vibrations with their antennae.

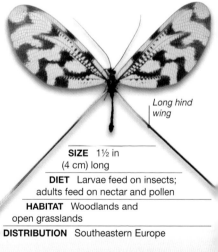

Long hind wing

SIZE	1½ in (4 cm) long
DIET	Larvae feed on insects; adults feed on nectar and pollen
HABITAT	Woodlands and open grasslands
DISTRIBUTION	Southeastern Europe

Owlfly
Libelloides macaronius

Owlflies can often be seen flying on warm sunny days, particularly during twilight. Adults are agile fliers and can catch flying insect prey in midair.

SIZE	1¼ in (3 cm) long
DIET	Other insects
HABITAT	Grasslands and warm, dry woodlands
DISTRIBUTION	Southern and central Europe, and Asia

Antlion
Palpares libelluloides

Antlions are slender insects that look like damselflies. Their larvae dig cone-shaped pits in sandy soil to trap ants and other small insects.

Organ in male for clasping female

SIZE	2–2¼ in (5–5.5 cm) long
DIET	Pollen, small insects, and spiders
HABITAT	Rough grasslands and warm scrubby regions
DISTRIBUTION	Mediterranean region

Mantisfly
Mantispa styriaca

The mantisfly belongs to a family of insects called mantispids. Their front legs resemble those of mantises and are used to grab prey. This insect's body has bright colors that deter predators.

When capturing prey, the mantisfly's lightning-fast strike takes just 60 milliseconds.

SIZE	½ in (1.4 cm) long
DIET	Small flies
HABITAT	Woodlands
DISTRIBUTION	Southern and central Europe

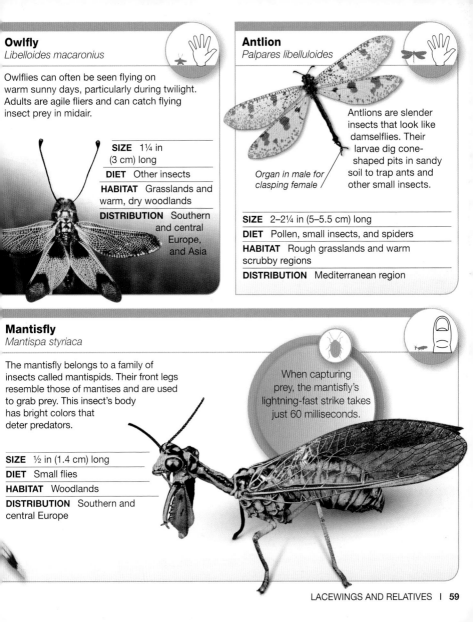

Beetles

This group forms the largest order of insect, Coleoptera, which contains about 370,000 species. Beetles are found in many habitats on land and in fresh water. They have tough front wings, called elytra, which fold over their thinner hind wings like a protective case.

Beetles range in size from tiny insects to tropical giants.

▲ The adult male titan beetle is 6½ in (17 cm) long and is one of the largest of all beetles.

▲ At about ¹⁄₃₂ in (0.6–0.7 mm) long, *Actidium coarctatum* is one of the smallest beetles in the world.

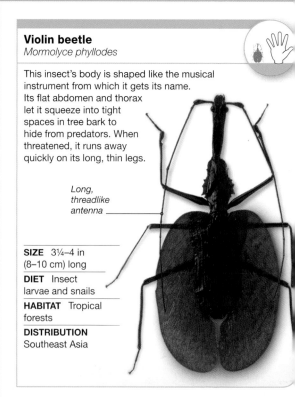

Violin beetle
Mormolyce phyllodes

This insect's body is shaped like the musical instrument from which it gets its name. Its flat abdomen and thorax let it squeeze into tight spaces in tree bark to hide from predators. When threatened, it runs away quickly on its long, thin legs.

Long, threadlike antenna

SIZE 3¼–4 in (8–10 cm) long

DIET Insect larvae and snails

HABITAT Tropical forests

DISTRIBUTION Southeast Asia

Great diving beetle
Dytiscus marginalis

When in water, these beetles breathe air stored under their wing cases. Their hairy legs propel them quickly through the water, but occasionally they float up, tail first, to add to their air supply.

SIZE   1⅓–1½ in (3.5–4 cm) long

DIET   Small aquatic invertebrates, fish, and tadpoles

HABITAT   Ponds and shallow lakes in tundra regions, wetlands, and urban areas

DISTRIBUTION   Europe and northern Asia

Bombardier beetle
Brachinus crepitans

The bombardier beetle has a unique way of defending itself. When threatened, it releases puffs of a hot scalding acid, with a loud popping sound. It can move its tail under its body and to either side to spray acid on a predator.

SIZE   ½–⅓ in (0.6–0.9 cm) long

DIET   Larvae of other beetles

HABITAT   Woodlands and grasslands

DISTRIBUTION   Europe

Devil's coach horse
Staphylinus olens

Unlike other beetles, whose bodies are fully covered by their wing cases, part of this beetle's abdomen is exposed. If disturbed, it curves its abdomen upward like a scorpion about to sting, which scares off predators. It can also run fast and gets its name from its speed and an Irish myth in which it was believed to be the devil in disguise, out to eat sinners.

SIZE   1¼ in (3 cm) long

DIET   Other insects

HABITAT   Woodlands and garden leaf litter

DISTRIBUTION   Europe, North America, and Australia

Minotaur beetle
Typhaeus typhoeus

Male and female minotaur beetles work together to dig tunnels in sandy soil for their nests. They also cooperate when feeding their young—the males gather the droppings of sheep and rabbits, which the females then shape into small, sausage-shaped portions for the larvae to eat.

SIZE ½–¾ in (1.5–2 cm) long

DIET Sheep and rabbit droppings

HABITAT Sandy areas in shrublands

DISTRIBUTION Western Europe

— Horn

Male beetles have bull-like horns like those on a minotaur—a half-man, half-bull creature in Greek mythology.

Hercules beetle
Dynastes hercules

Relative to its size, this beetle is one of the strongest creatures on Earth. It can carry 850 times its own body weight—this feat of strength is equal to a human carrying 12 buses.

SIZE 2½–6½ in (6–17 cm) long

DIET Larvae feed on decaying organic matter; adults feed on rotting fruit

HABITAT Rainforests

DISTRIBUTION Central and South America

Gold beetle
Chrysina esplendens

The beetle's color does not come from a gold or yellow pigment on its body, but is due to its elytra reflecting sunlight in a way that makes it look like polished metal. The glinting shine often confuses predators in the dark forests in which the gold beetle lives.

Strong claws

Stag beetle
Lucanus cervus

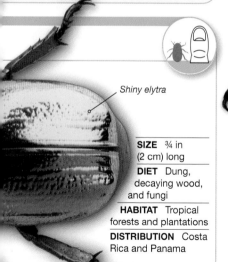

The stag beetle lays eggs in the decaying stumps or roots of trees. It spends 3–7 years as a larva, feeding on rotting wood, before pupating in cells of chewed wood fibres.

SIZE ⅞–3 in (2.2–7.5 cm) long

DIET Larvae feed on decaying wood; adults feed on oozing sap or fallen fruit

HABITAT Deciduous woodlands

DISTRIBUTION Southern and central Europe

Shiny elytra

SIZE ¾ in (2 cm) long

DIET Dung, decaying wood, and fungi

HABITAT Tropical forests and plantations

DISTRIBUTION Costa Rica and Panama

Flower chafer
Neptunides polychrous

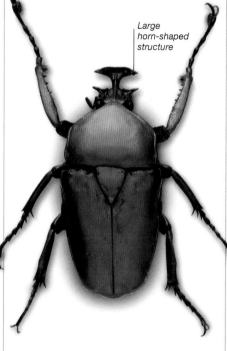

These beetles are robust, with square, flattish bodies. They have hornlike projections on their head and spines on their legs. Flower chafers are generally green, but the body color can vary.

Large horn-shaped structure

SIZE 1¼–1½ in (3–3.5 cm) long

DIET Larvae feed on dead wood; adults feed on pollen, nectar, and fruit

HABITAT Tropical forests

DISTRIBUTION East Africa

Common red soldier beetle
Rhagonycha fulva

Adults of this species can be found on top of fully bloomed flowers, where they feed on nectar and other insects. The larvae live in the soil and leaf litter, eating other small invertebrates, such as springtails, aphids, and fly larvae.

SIZE ½ in (1 cm) long

DIET Larvae eat small soil-dwelling invertebrates; adults feed on pollen and nectar

HABITAT Meadows and margins of woodlands

DISTRIBUTION Europe and North America

Red-spotted longhorn beetle
Batocera rufomaculata

This beetle's larvae tunnel through trees, eating away at the wood. They are known to attack mango and fig trees, which is why the insect is also called the mango borer or fig borer.

SIZE 2–2½ in (5–6 cm) long

DIET Larvae feed on wood; adults feed on sap, pollen, nectar, and leaves

HABITAT On ground, in soil, and in leaf litter in tropical forests and plantations

DISTRIBUTION India and Southeast Asia

Larder beetle
Dermestes lardarius

Larder beetles lay their eggs in the flesh and bones of dead and decaying animals. In houses, they infest stored food, especially animal products, such as ham, bacon, and cheese.

SIZE ⅓–½ in (8–10 mm) long

DIET Animal remains, dried meat, stored cheese, fur, hair, bones, and abandoned nests of birds

HABITAT Buildings, houses, and woodlands

DISTRIBUTION Worldwide except polar regions

Yellow longhorn beetle
Phosphorus jansoni

Like other longhorn beetles, this has very long antennae—longer, in fact, than its entire body. It is also brightly colored and is often spotted on cola trees, which are attacked by its larvae.

SIZE 1¼–1½ in (2.8–3.6 cm) long

DIET Larvae feed on wood; adults feed on sap, nectar, and leaves

HABITAT Tropical forests

DISTRIBUTION West Africa

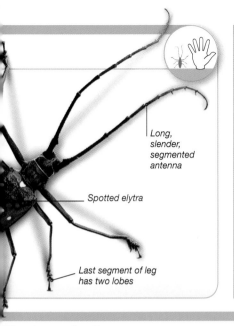

Long, slender, segmented antenna

Spotted elytra

Last segment of leg has two lobes

Sexton beetle
Nicrophorus investigator

Using its antennae, this beetle is able to sense dead animals from a distance. After it finds a carcass, usually that of a small mouse or bird, the beetle buries it in the ground. Eggs are then laid on the decaying animal, which provides food for the larvae when they hatch.

SIZE 1 in (2.6 cm) long

DIET Dead and decaying animals

HABITAT Woodlands and grasslands

DISTRIBUTION
Northern
hemisphere

Blue fungus beetle
Gibbifer californicus

These shiny, black-spotted beetles are very common during the summer, especially in the rainy season. They are often seen feeding on patches of fungi on tall trees.

SIZE ¾–1 in (1.8–2.2 cm) long

DIET Fungi on live trees or decaying wood

HABITAT Moist woodlands

DISTRIBUTION Southwestern US

Seven-spot ladybug
Coccinella septempunctata

This is one of the most common beetles in Europe. Its bright elytra warns predators that it is poisonous. To deter its attackers further, it oozes its foul-tasting blood from its leg joints.

SIZE ¼–⅓ in (6–9 mm) long

DIET Soft-bodied insects, such as aphids

HABITAT Woods, parks, and gardens

DISTRIBUTION Europe, Asia, and North America

Twenty-two spot ladybug
Psyllobora vigintiduopunctata

Most ladybugs are short-legged with brightly colored bodies, which are spotted or striped. Twenty-two spots dot the elytra of this small beetle—11 on each forewing.

SIZE ⅛–¼ in (3–5 mm) long

DIET Fungi, such as mildews

HABITAT Meadows

DISTRIBUTION Europe

Tortoise beetle
Aspidomorpha miliaris

A tortoise beetle's body is covered by a shieldlike "shell." Like a tortoise, this insect withdraws its head and feet under its shell when threatened. It then firmly attaches its shell to a leaf.

SIZE ⅝ in (15 mm) long

DIET Plants of the *Ipomea* genus

HABITAT Corn and sweet potato plantations

DISTRIBUTION Southeast Asia

Circular "shell"

Jeweled frog beetle
Sagra buqueti

Strong hind legs similar to those of a frog have inspired the name of this beetle. The way its elytra reflect sunlight make it look like a green-red jewel.

SIZE 1¼–1½ in (3–3.5 cm) long

DIET Larvae feed on stems, foliage, and roots; adults feed on leaves

HABITAT Tropical forests

DISTRIBUTION Thailand and Malaysia

Black oil beetle
Meloe proscarabaeus

Black oil beetles lay eggs on flowers visited by bees. After hatching, the larvae attach themselves to bees and hitch a ride to the nest, where they feed on the larvae of the bees.

SIZE 1–1½ in (2.4–3.4 cm) long

DIET Larvae feed on pollen, nectar, and bee larvae; adults feed on plants and nectar

HABITAT Warm meadows, heaths, and coastal areas

DISTRIBUTION Europe

Click beetle
Chalcolepidius limbatus

Powerful muscles in the thorax of the click beetle jerk suddenly to propel it into the air. As it leaps, the insect makes a loud "click" sound, which frightens its predators.

SIZE 1¼–1½ in (3–4 cm) long

DIET Larvae feed on plant roots, tubers, and other insects; adults feed on other insects and plant matter

HABITAT Woodlands and grasslands

DISTRIBUTION South America

Fog-basking darkling beetle
Onymacris candidipennis

As moisture-laden fog rolls in from the Atlantic Ocean, this beetle lowers its head and raises its elytra. Droplets of water from the fog then collect on its forewings and drip into its mouth. This amazing technique helps it collect enough water to survive in the Namib Desert.

SIZE ¾ in (1.8–2 cm) long

DIET Larvae feed on plant roots; adults eat decaying organic matter

HABITAT Deserts

DISTRIBUTION Southwestern coast of Africa

Ant beetle
Thanasimus formicarius

Ant beetles hunt bark beetles and their larvae on dead and fallen coniferous trees. They use their strong mandibles to attack their tough prey. Ant beetles can move quickly when on the hunt.

SIZE ¼–½ in (7–10 mm) long

DIET Bark beetles, larvae, and eggs

HABITAT Coniferous forests

DISTRIBUTION Europe and northern Asia

Giraffe-necked weevil
Trachelophorus giraffa

This strange-looking weevil gets its name from its very long, giraffelike neck. The neck is 2–3 times longer in males than in females. The males use their long necks for head-bobbing contests to impress females. The females use their shorter necks to roll leaves into tubes, laying a single egg in each tube.

Jewel weevil
Eupholus linnei

Beetles of the Curculionidae family are also called weevils. The heads of these insects are extended to form a structure called the rostrum, which carries the mandibles. This weevil uses its mandibles to chew through its favorite food—yams (the starch-rich tubers of some climbing plants).

SIZE ¼–1 in (2–2.6 cm) long

DIET Plant tubers

HABITAT Woodlands and grasslands

DISTRIBUTION Eastern Indonesia

Segmented antenna on small head

The giraffe-necked weevil has the longest neck of any insect.

SIZE 1 in (2.6 cm) long

DIET Plant matter

HABITAT Rainforests

DISTRIBUTION Madagascar

In medieval times, people believed that stag beetles carried hot embers in their jaws, causing

house fires

STAG BEETLE

Battles between male stag beetles are common during the mating season. Rivals wrestle each other for females or for territory. They grab one another with their powerful mandibles, which look like the antlers of stags.

Scorpionflies and fleas

A slim, scorpionlike abdomen is a feature of all 550 species of scorpionfly that form the order Mecoptera. They are either predators or scavengers of decaying matter. In contrast, the 2,400 species of flea are all parasites of mammals or birds and suck on their blood. They make up the order Siphonaptera.

Common scorpionfly
Panorpa communis

Slender antenna

Downward-pointing beak

Mottled wing

The wings of common scorpionflies are not very strong, and so they rarely fly very far. They can be spotted resting on leaves between May and September. The males have a pair of upturned claspers at the tips of their abdomens, which look like the sting of a scorpion. They use the claspers to grab females during mating.

SIZE ¾ in (1.8 cm) long

DIET Larvae feed on decaying organic matter; adults feed on live and dead insects

HABITAT Shady hedgerows and margins of woodlands

DISTRIBUTION Western Europe

Snow scorpionfly
Boreus hyemalis

This insect lives at high altitudes, often in snowy conditions. Its short, nonfunctional wings are hairlike in the males and scalelike in the females. Although the snow scorpionfly does not fly, it can jump short distances using its strong hind and middle legs.

SIZE ⅛–¼ in (3–5 mm) long

DIET Mosses

HABITAT Cold and mountainous regions

DISTRIBUTION Europe

Rabbit flea
Spilopsyllus cuniculi

Special rubbery pads on the hind legs store energy and help these wingless fleas to leap onto host animals. Rabbit fleas are found near the ears of rabbits. They feed on rabbit blood, but can survive for many months away from their host.

SIZE Under ⅛ in (3 mm) long

DIET Blood of rabbits

HABITAT On rabbits and wild hares

DISTRIBUTION Northern hemisphere

Cat flea
Ctenocephalides felis

These fleas are usually found on domestic cats. Although a single cat may have only a few adult fleas feeding on it, thousands of flea larvae may live where the cat rests. Hungry cat fleas can leap up to a distance of 13½ in (34 cm) and will bite humans.

SIZE ⅛ in (3 mm) long

DIET Blood of mammals, such as cats, dogs, and humans

HABITAT On cats

DISTRIBUTION Worldwide except polar regions

True flies

These insects belong to the order Diptera and have only a single pair of wings. Their hind wings have evolved into organs called halteres that help with balance during flight. There are about 150,000 species in this order.

True flies play important roles as pollinators, predators, and decomposers.

▲ Hover flies visit flowers to suck nectar. Grains of pollen stick to their bodies and are dispersed to other flowers, pollinating them.

▲ Parasitoid flies lay eggs on caterpillars, which are crop pests. The fly grubs eat the caterpillars from inside and emerge to form chrysalises (as shown above).

Fungus gnat
Platyura marginata

Small, delicate, and mosquitolike in appearance, this species is commonly found in human settlements, usually near plants in houses.

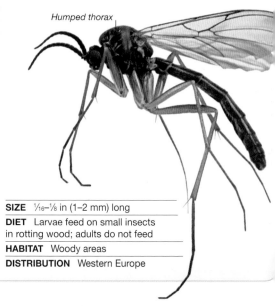

Humped thorax

SIZE	$\frac{1}{16}$–$\frac{1}{8}$ in (1–2 mm) long
DIET	Larvae feed on small insects in rotting wood; adults do not feed
HABITAT	Woody areas
DISTRIBUTION	Western Europe

Farmyard midge
Culicoides nubeculosus

Also called a biting midge, the farmyard midge has strong, short legs and piercing mouthparts that help it to suck blood. A bite from this insect can cause irritation to the skin.

SIZE 3/16 in (2 mm) long

DIET Larvae feed on other insects and plants; adults feed on the blood of horses and cattle

HABITAT In dung or sewage

DISTRIBUTION Europe

Mouthparts help in sucking blood from host

Mosquito
Culex sp.

The most dangerous pests in the world, female mosquitoes spread many deadly diseases, including malaria. They pierce the skin of large animals with syringelike mouthparts and feed on their blood. Females of the *Culex* genus spread diseases such as Japanese encephalitis and filariasis.

Long hind leg

SIZE 1/4–1/3 in (6–9 mm) long

DIET Males feed on flowers; females feed on the blood of mammals and birds

HABITAT Near water, in warm and humid tropical regions

DISTRIBUTION Worldwide except polar regions

Long proboscis (syringelike mouthpart)

Apple maggot
Rhagoletis pomonella

The apple maggot is a fruit fly. It is an apple pest but also attacks other fruits. Female flies lay their eggs in unripe fruit, and the larvae eat the fruit from the core. This causes the fruit to decay, making it unsuitable for humans to eat.

SIZE ¼ in (5 mm) long

DIET Fruit

HABITAT Orchards

DISTRIBUTION North America

Distinct black and white stripes on wing

Stalk-eyed fly
Achias rothschildi

Long eye stalk

Dance fly
Empis tessellata

Mating swarms of this species fly around in a "dance." As part of the mating ritual, the males court the females by offering dead prey as food.

SIZE ½ in (1–1.2 cm) long

DIET Larvae feed on soft-bodied prey; adults feed on small flies and nectar

HABITAT Meadows and hedgerows

DISTRIBUTION Europe and Asia

These flies are usually found at an altitude of 4,500 ft (1,400 m). Males have distinctive long eye stalks, which help them to attract mates. Males with shorter eye stalks tend to be submissive when fighting with other males.

SIZE ⅝–¾ in (1.5–1.8 cm) long

DIET Larvae feed on other insects and decaying organic matter; adults do not feed

HABITAT Tropical forests

DISTRIBUTION Papua New Guinea

Drone fly
Eristalis tenax

This insect belongs to the family of hover flies. The drone fly looks like the stinging honey bee and flies like the bee as well, but does not have a stinger. The resemblance helps to ward off predators.

SIZE ½ in (1.1–1.3 cm) long

DIET Pollen and nectar

HABITAT Grasslands, woodlands, mountains, deserts, and tropical forests

DISTRIBUTION Europe; introduced to North America

Giant blue robber fly
Blepharotes splendidissimus

Platelike tuft of hair

Stout leg

Giant blue robber flies have a sharp, forward-pointing proboscis (long, sucking mouthpart), which they use to stab prey and inject a paralyzing saliva. They then suck up the body fluids of the disabled prey.

SIZE 1½–2 in (3.5–5 cm) long

DIET Beetles and flies; larvae also eat decaying matter

HABITAT Tropical and subtropical regions

DISTRIBUTION Eastern Australia

Bluebottle
Calliphora vicina

These are often the first flies to arrive at the bodies of dead animals, including humans. They breed in the decaying flesh, where their whitish larvae, called maggots, grow quickly.

SIZE ½ in (1–1.2 cm) long

DIET Larvae feed on decaying carcasses; adults feed on nectar and liquids from rotting organic matter

HABITAT On and near decaying organic matter

DISTRIBUTION Europe and North America

Flesh fly
Sarcophaga carnaria

Flesh flies breed in decaying carcasses and even inside of wounds on mammals. They are ovoviviparous—larvae hatch from eggs inside the body of the female before emerging.

SIZE ½–¾ in (1.4–1.8 cm) long

DIET Larvae feed on decaying carcasses; adults feed on nectar and liquids from rotting matter

HABITAT On and near decaying organic matter

DISTRIBUTION Europe and Asia

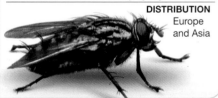

Yellow dung fly
Scathophaga stercoraria

As the name suggests, these flies are often spotted on the dung of cattle and horses. The dung serves as their breeding ground and provides food for the growing larvae. The adults, however, are predatory and hunt other insects attracted to the dung.

SIZE ⅓–½ in (8–11 mm) long

DIET Larvae feed on dung; adults prey on other insects

HABITAT On and near animal dung

DISTRIBUTION Northern hemisphere

Bristles cover the entire body

House fly
Musca domestica

Common in homes around the world, the house fly seems quite harmless, but can spread bacterial and viral diseases while it feeds. It uses its spongelike mouthparts to lap up liquids easily. When feeding on solid food, it uses its saliva to soften the food before eating.

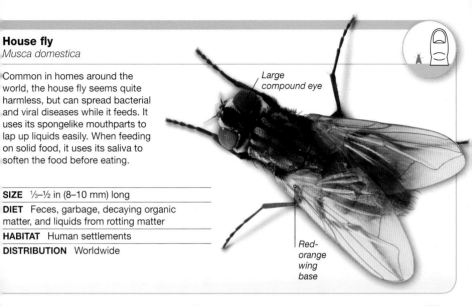

Large compound eye

Red-orange wing base

SIZE ⅓–½ in (8–10 mm) long

DIET Feces, garbage, decaying organic matter, and liquids from rotting matter

HABITAT Human settlements

DISTRIBUTION Worldwide

Forest fly
Hippobosca equina

The forest fly is a parasite of horses and other animals. Once it finds a host, it grabs on tightly with its claws and is difficult to remove. It uses its piercing mouthparts to suck blood.

SIZE ⅓ in (8 mm) long

DIET Larvae are nourished inside the mother's body before emerging; adults feed on blood from horses, deer, and cattle

HABITAT Woodlands

DISTRIBUTION Europe and Asia

Savanna tsetse fly
Glossina morsitans

Well-developed biting mouthparts are used by the tsetse fly to feed on the blood of a number of mammals, including humans, antelope, cattle, horses, and pigs. In humans, the fly spreads diseases, such as elephantiasis and sleeping sickness.

SIZE ⅓–½ in (0.9–1.4 cm) long

DIET Larvae are nourished inside the mother's body before emerging; adults feed on mammal blood

HABITAT Savanna, grasslands, and farmlands

DISTRIBUTION Africa

ROBBER FLY
The robber fly is a good hunter. With its flexible neck, it can turn its head to look directly at its prey. It often chases flying insects, steering skillfully with its long, narrow wings. It uses its spiny legs to grab prey midair, which it then pierces with its powerful beak.

With as many as

8,000
lenses

in each compound
eye, the robber fly has
extremely clear vision

Caddisflies

Mothlike in appearance, caddisflies have slim, hairy bodies and long, thin antennae. They are abundant in freshwater habitats, where their aquatic larvae often build themselves protective cases. About 13,000 species of caddisfly make up the order Trichoptera.

Mottled sedge
Glyphotaelius pellucidus

The mottled sedge breeds around ponds and lakes. The females lay eggs coated with a jellylike substance and stick them on leaves hanging above the surface of water. When the eggs are ready to hatch, they fall into the water, where the larvae emerge. The larvae make a protective case out of pieces of dead leaves.

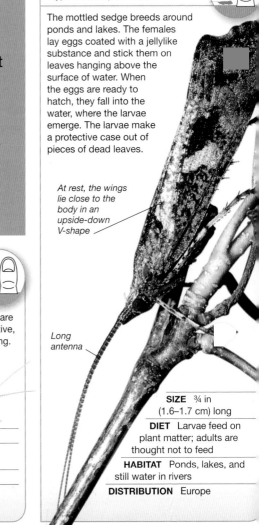

At rest, the wings lie close to the body in an upside-down V-shape

Long antenna

SIZE ¾ in (1.6–1.7 cm) long

DIET Larvae feed on plant matter; adults are thought not to feed

HABITAT Ponds, lakes, and still water in rivers

DISTRIBUTION Europe

Salt and pepper microcaddis
Agraylea multipunctata

The larvae of this small caddisfly swim freely around their watery habitats until they are almost fully grown. They then build a protective, purselike cocoon of silk and sand for pupating.

SIZE ⅛–³⁄₁₆ in (3–4.5 mm) long

DIET Larvae feed on algae; adults are thought not to feed

HABITAT Ponds and lakes

DISTRIBUTION North America

Dark-spotted sedge
Philopotamus montanus

Caddisfly larvae cannot survive in polluted water, so their presence indicates good water quality.

Silk, sand, gravel, and plant materials are used by the larvae of this species to build protective underwater nets, which they attach to the undersides of rocks. Plant particles and algae filter through these nets, providing food for the growing larvae.

SIZE ½ in (1.1–1.3 cm) long

DIET Larvae feed on plant matter and algae; adults are thought not to feed

HABITAT Fast-flowing rocky streams

DISTRIBUTION Europe

Great red sedge
Phryganea grandis

This is the largest species of caddisfly in the UK. The females are smaller than the males and have a dark stripe on their forewings.

SIZE 1¼ in (3 cm) long

DIET Larvae feed on plant matter, other insects, small fish, and decaying organic matter; adults are thought not to feed

HABITAT Weedy lakes and slow-moving streams and rivers

DISTRIBUTION Europe

Marbled sedge
Hydropsyche contubernalis

Like the larvae of the dark-spotted sedge, the larvae of the marbled sedge also weave underwater nets. The nets protect the larvae and catch particles of food in the water.

SIZE ½ in (1.4 cm) long

DIET Larvae feed on plant matter and algae; adults are thought not to feed

HABITAT Streams and rivers

DISTRIBUTION Worldwide except polar regions

Moths and butterflies

The 165,000 species of moth and butterfly are members of the order Lepidoptera. Their bodies and wings are covered with many tiny colored scales.

Garden tiger
Arctia caja

This moth usually rests with its hind wings hidden under its forewings. If threatened, it flashes its bright hind wings and flies off. This helps it to startle and ward off predators.

SIZE 2–3 in (5–7.5 cm) wingspan

DIET Larvae feed on low-growing plants and shrubs; adults feed on nectar

HABITAT Woods, parks, and gardens

DISTRIBUTION Europe, North America, and Asia

Furry, brown thorax

Black spots on hind wings

◀ Like many moths, the Cecropia moth from North America has large, feathery antennae.

◀ Butterflies have thick-tipped, clublike antennae, as seen on this swallowtail butterfly.

Snout moth
Vitessa suradeva

Yellow and black color pattern on thorax

Unlike other related moths, the snout moth is brightly colored. The striking patterns on the wings and the flashy orange tip of the tail signal to predators that the moth has a foul taste.

SIZE 1½–2 in (4–5 cm) wingspan

DIET Caterpillars feed on the leaves of poisonous shrubs; adults do not feed

HABITAT Rainforests

DISTRIBUTION India, Southeast Asia, and New Guinea

Silk-worm moth
Bombyx mori

The larvae of butterflies and moths are called caterpillars. When the caterpillars of the silk-worm moth pupate, they cover themselves in a cocoon of raw silk produced from their salivary glands. This cocoon is used as the raw material for producing silk commercially. Silk-worm moths have been bred in captivity for thousands of years.

SIZE 1½–2½ in (4–6 cm) wingspan

DIET White mulberry leaves

HABITAT Bred in captivity; not found in the wild

DISTRIBUTION China; introduced worldwide

Giant agrippa
Thysania agrippina

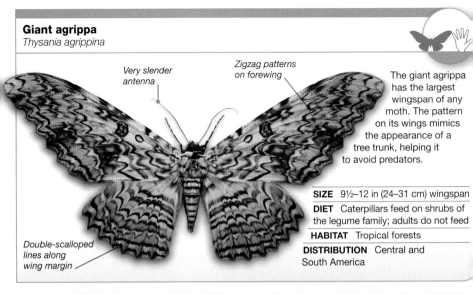

Very slender antenna

Zigzag patterns on forewing

The giant agrippa has the largest wingspan of any moth. The pattern on its wings mimics the appearance of a tree trunk, helping it to avoid predators.

Double-scalloped lines along wing margin

SIZE 9½–12 in (24–31 cm) wingspan

DIET Caterpillars feed on shrubs of the legume family; adults do not feed

HABITAT Tropical forests

DISTRIBUTION Central and South America

Coppery dysphania
Dysphania cuprina

The brilliant orange and black colors of this moth's wings indicates to birds that it tastes unpleasant. The moth also avoids predators by flying during the day with other similarly colored butterflies, such as the Oriental monarch.

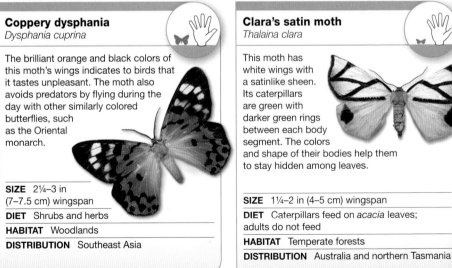

SIZE 2¼–3 in (7–7.5 cm) wingspan

DIET Shrubs and herbs

HABITAT Woodlands

DISTRIBUTION Southeast Asia

Clara's satin moth
Thalaina clara

This moth has white wings with a satinlike sheen. Its caterpillars are green with darker green rings between each body segment. The colors and shape of their bodies help them to stay hidden among leaves.

SIZE 1¼–2 in (4–5 cm) wingspan

DIET Caterpillars feed on *acacia* leaves; adults do not feed

HABITAT Temperate forests

DISTRIBUTION Australia and northern Tasmania

American Moon moth
Actias luna

Adult American Moon moths live for only a week. During this time, they usually fly at night. They have very long, tapering hind wings, which look like long tails. The wings have large spots that confuse predators, who mistake them for the eyes of larger creatures.

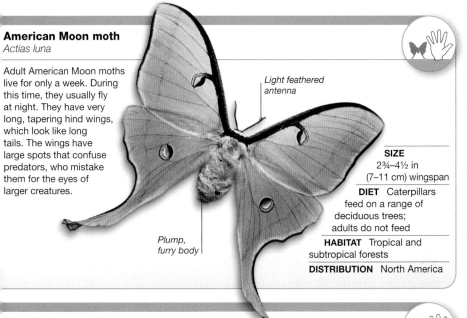

Light feathered antenna

Plump, furry body

SIZE
2¾–4½ in
(7–11 cm) wingspan

DIET Caterpillars feed on a range of deciduous trees; adults do not feed

HABITAT Tropical and subtropical forests

DISTRIBUTION North America

Wallich's owl moth
Brahmaea wallichii

The Wallich's owl moth gets its name from the large spots at the base of its forewings that resemble an owl's eyes. Adults rest on tree trunks or on the ground during the day, and the dull brown color of their wings blends with the color of the trunks and the soil.

SIZE 4–6½ in (10–16 cm) wingspan

DIET Caterpillars feed on the leaves of trees and bushes; adults do not feed

HABITAT Tropical and temperate forests

DISTRIBUTION Northern India, China, and Japan

Large spot on forewing

The caterpillars of this moth have strange extendable stalks sticking out from their heads and tails.

White plume moth
Pterophorus pentadactyla

The wings of this distinctive moth are divided into fine, feathery segments. These are clearly visible when the moth holds its wings to the sides while resting.

SIZE 1–1¼ in (2.5–3 cm) wingspan

DIET Caterpillars feed on hedge bindweed; adults feed on nectar

HABITAT Dry grasslands, waste grounds, and gardens

DISTRIBUTION Europe

Elephant hawk moth
Deilephila elpenor

Pointed forewing

Hornet moth
Sesia apiforms

Yellow and brown stripes on the body, transparent wings, and a pointed abdomen help the hornet moth to mimic the appearance of a sting-bearing hornet. Predators tend to leave them alone, fearing a sting.

SIZE 1¼–1¾ in (3–4.5 cm) wingspan

DIET
Caterpillars bore into the trunks of willow and poplar trees; adults do not feed

HABITAT Temperate forests

DISTRIBUTION Europe and Asia

Six-spot burnet
Zygaena filipendulae

This insect is most likely to be seen flying on hot days between June and August. Six bright red spots are clearly visible on each wing when it flies. These warn predators that the moth is poisonous.

SIZE 1–1½ in (2.5–3.8 cm) wingspan

DIET Caterpillars feed on bird's foot trefoil and clover; adults feed on nectar

HABITAT Meadows and woodlands

DISTRIBUTION Europe and Asia

Hawk moths are fast fliers. The spectacularly colored adults of this species are often seen in early summer. The moth is named for its caterpillars, which have eyelike marks on their bodies. The marks become prominent when a caterpillar expands the back of its head. This makes the front part of its body look like an elephant's trunk.

SIZE 2¼–2½ in (5.5–6 cm) wingspan

DIET Caterpillars feed on bedstraw and willow herbs; adults feed on nectar

HABITAT Temperate lowlands

DISTRIBUTION Europe and Asia

Dark margin on hind wing

Madagascan sunset moth
Chrysiridia rhipheus

In 19th-century England, the colorful wings of this moth were used to make jewelry.

Pointed forewing

Hind wing has three tail-like structures

When this moth was discovered, scientists mistook it for a butterfly because of the brilliant colors of the adults. Its caterpillars are not harmed by the toxins in the shrubs they feed on.

SIZE 3–3¾ in (7.5–9.5 cm) wingspan

DIET Shrubs of the spurge family

HABITAT Woodlands and forests

DISTRIBUTION Madagascar

Indian leaf butterfly
Kallima inachus

The upper surface of this butterfly's wings are brilliantly colored, while the undersides are dull brown and look like a dry leaf. When it rests, its wings are folded in such a way that only the undersides are visible. This often saves the butterfly from predators, since they mistake it for a dead leaf.

SIZE 3½–4¾ in (9–12 cm) wingspan

DIET Larvae feed on plants; adults feed on juices of rotting fruit

HABITAT Tropical forests

DISTRIBUTION Southeast Asia, between India and Japan

Pointed forewing

Tail-like structure on hind wing

Monarch butterfly
Danaus plexippus

Known for their spectacular long-distance migrations, some monarch butterflies undertake an incredible journey of 2,800 miles (4,500 km) from Canada to Mexico in the late summer. They fly back north in the spring.

SIZE 3–4 in (7.5–10 cm) wingspan

DIET Caterpillars feed on milkweed plants; adults feed on nectar

HABITAT Fields, meadows, and gardens

DISTRIBUTION North America, New Zealand, Australia, Canary Islands, and Pacific islands

Owl butterfly
Caligo idomeneus

The owl butterfly has large spots on the undersides of its hind wings that look like eyes. Many predators get scared of these spots and leave the butterfly alone.

SIZE 4¾–6 in (12–15 cm) wingspan

DIET Leaves of banana plants

HABITAT Tropical forests

DISTRIBUTION South America

Common morpho
Morpho peleides

Millions of tiny scales lining the upper surface of this butterfly's wings reflect sunlight in a particular way to produce a brilliant blue color. However, the undersides of the wings are brown and help the butterfly to blend in with its surroundings, making it almost invisible to predators. When it flies, it beats its wings and flashes the blue and brown colors. Predators get confused because it seems to appear and disappear in flight.

SIZE 3¾–6 in (9.5–15 cm) wingspan

DIET Larvae feed on plants; adults feed on juices of rotting fruit

HABITAT Tropical forests

DISTRIBUTION Central and South America

Green dragontail
Lamproptera meges

While flying, the green dragontail beats its wings rapidly, allowing it to dart in different directions or even hover in one place. Its long tails and rapid flight make it look like a dragonfly.

SIZE 1½–2 in (4–5 cm) wingspan

DIET Larvae feed on leaves; adults feed on nectar

HABITAT Tropical forests

DISTRIBUTION South and Southeast Asia

Spanish festoon
Zerynthia rumina

Zigzag wing pattern warns off predators

Queen Alexandra's birdwing
Ornithoptera alexandrae

Females have broader wings

All birdwings are large, but this endangered species is the largest butterfly in the world. The females are larger than the males and have brown and yellow markings. Only the males are bright blue and green.

SIZE 8–12 in (20–31 cm) wingspan

DIET Larvae feed on leaves; adults feed on nectar

HABITAT Tropical forests

DISTRIBUTION Forests of the Oro province in southeastern Papua New Guinea

The caterpillars of the Spanish festoon deter predators by releasing an unpleasant fluid from an organ behind their head. The adults can also ward off predators—their striking colors dazzle the attacker, leaving them confused about where to strike.

SIZE 1¾–2 in (4.5–5 cm) wingspan

DIET Larvae feed on birthwort plants; adults feed on nectar

HABITAT Scrublands and meadows

DISTRIBUTION Southeastern France, Spain, Portugal, and northern Africa

Cleopatra
Gonepteryx cleopatra

The green caterpillars of this species transform into yellowish adults. The females are the color of straw, while the males are bright yellow and orange.

SIZE 2–2¾ in (5–7 cm) wingspan

DIET Larvae feed on buckthorn; adults feed on the nectar of knapweed and thistles

HABITAT Open woods and scrublands

DISTRIBUTION Southern Europe, northern Africa, and Turkey

Black-veined white
Aporia crataegi

Black veins on whitish wings make this butterfly easy to identify. The wings of the females tend to be more transparent than those of the males.

SIZE 2¼–3 in (5.5–7.5 cm) wingspan

DIET Larvae feed on blackthorn and hawthorn; adults feed on nectar

HABITAT Orchards and bushes

DISTRIBUTION Europe, northern Africa, and Asia

Tiger pierid
Dismorphia amphione

Tiger pierid butterflies are commonly seen flying along the edges of forests. The black and orange patterns on their wings mimic similarly colored, but foul-tasting, butterflies.

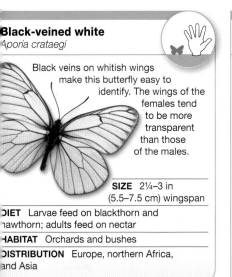

SIZE 1½–1¾ in (4–4.5 cm)

DIET Caterpillars feed on plants; adults feed on nectar

HABITAT Tropical forests

DISTRIBUTION Southern Mexico, the Caribbean, and northern South America

Hewitson's blue hairstreak
Evenus coronata

The distinct black border on the wings of this butterfly is darker in the females. The blue color of the wing is also brighter in the females, and only the females have a red patch on their hind wings.

SIZE 1¾–2½ in (4.5–6 cm) wingspan

DIET Caterpillars feed on plants and small insects; adults feed on nectar

HABITAT Tropical forests

DISTRIBUTION South America

Tail-like structure on hind wing

Duke of Burgundy fritillary
Hamearis lucina

The easiest way to tell the difference between the males and females of this species is to count the legs—females have six, while males have only four. The males are also much more aggressive, fighting each other for territory.

Bright orange spots are typical of this species

SIZE 1¼–1½ in (3–4 cm) wingspan

DIET Cowslip and primrose

HABITAT Flower meadows, grasslands, and woodlands

DISTRIBUTION Central Europe

Sonoran blue
Philotes sonorensis

Scales on the wings reflect sunlight in a particular way, giving the wings their metallic blue color

This spectacularly colored butterfly is active early in the year and is often spotted flying through the canyons of the Sierra Nevada mountains. It is one of the few blue-colored butterflies to have orange spots on the upper surface of its wings.

SIZE	¼–1 in (2–2.5 cm) wingspan
DIET	Stonecrops
HABITAT	Rocky cliffs and creeks in deserts
DISTRIBUTION	Southwestern US

The cocoons of the Atlas moth are so big, they are used in Taiwan as
purses

ATLAS MOTH
The males of this species, one of the largest moths in the world, have broad, feathery, comblike antennae. Special receptors on each antenna help the male to detect pheromones (scent chemicals) released by the females—even from several miles away.

FOCUS ON...
HONEY BEES

A honey bee society is divided into drones, female workers, and a queen.

▲ Drones are male bees that mate with the queen. There can be a few hundred drones in a hive.

▲ Worker bees are females that cannot reproduce. They build the hive and make honey. There can be 80,000 workers in a hive.

▲ In each colony, only one female grows into the queen. She mates with several drones and lays up to 2,000 eggs in a day.

Sawflies, wasps, bees, and ants

Sawflies, wasps, bees, and ants number around 150,000 species and make up the order Hymenoptera. Bees and ants are mostly social and live in colonies.

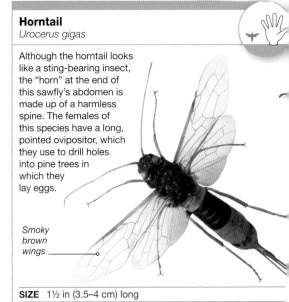

Horntail
Urocerus gigas

Although the horntail looks like a sting-bearing insect, the "horn" at the end of this sawfly's abdomen is made up of a harmless spine. The females of this species have a long, pointed ovipositor, which they use to drill holes into pine trees in which they lay eggs.

Smoky brown wings

SIZE	1½ in (3.5–4 cm) long
DIET	Fungus and wood
HABITAT	Deciduous, coniferous, and temperate forests
DISTRIBUTION	Europe, Asia, northern Africa, and North America

Oak apple gall wasp
Biorhiza pallida

The females of this species lay their eggs on the leaf buds of oak trees. After the larvae hatch, they release chemicals into the tree, which leads to the formation of galls (hard, lumpy growths of plant tissue) around the larvae. The galls provide food and protection.

SIZE ⅛–¼ in (5–6.5 mm) long

DIET Larvae feed on gall tissue; adults are thought not to feed

HABITAT Oak trees

DISTRIBUTION Europe and Asia

Stem sawfly
Cephus nigrinus

Stem sawflies are serious pests of crops. The females use their sawlike ovipositor to cut into the stems of grasses and lay eggs in the slits. Once the larvae hatch, they bore downward inside the stems, feeding rapidly.

SIZE ¼–⅓ in (7–9 mm) long

DIET Stems of grasses

HABITAT Pastures, meadows, and farms

DISTRIBUTION Western Europe

Leaf-rolling sawfly
Acantholyda erythrocephala

Female leaf-rolling sawflies deposit their eggs on leaves. After hatching, the larvae feed on the leaves and produce a chemical that causes the leaves to roll into tubes, which provide shelter for the larvae.

SIZE ¼–⅓ in (7–9 mm) long

DIET Leaves of plants

HABITAT Temperate forests

DISTRIBUTION Europe, Asia, and Canada

Tiphiid wasp
Methoca ichneumonides

The wingless females hunt the ground-dwelling larvae of scarab, longhorn, and tiger beetles. They sting the larvae to paralyze them before laying a single egg on each larva. When the wasp larvae hatch, they have a source of food.

SIZE ⅓–½ in (9–11 mm) long

DIET Larvae are parasites on beetle larvae; adults feed on nectar

HABITAT Sandy areas

DISTRIBUTION Europe

Braconid wasp
Bathyaulax sp.

Braconid wasps lay eggs on hosts, such as caterpillars and the larvae of beetles and flies. After the wasp larvae hatch, they feed on the hosts and most pupate inside their hosts.

SIZE ⅛–½ in (3–10 mm) long

DIET Larvae are parasitoids on caterpillars and larvae of beetles and flies; adults feed on nectar

HABITAT Forests, woodlands, and grasslands

DISTRIBUTION Africa and Southeast Asia

European hornet
Vespa crabro

This wasp is a social insect and lives in colonies made up of workers, males, and a queen. European hornet colonies have only a few hundred workers. These wasps build their nests in hollow trees.

SIZE 1–1½ in (2.5–3.5 cm) long

DIET Other insects, fallen fruit, and carrion

HABITAT Woodlands

DISTRIBUTION Europe and Asia

Splendid emerald wasp
Stilbum splendidum

The bright metallic green color of this wasp's body makes it look like an emerald. Its hard body surface protects it from the stings of bees and other wasps.

SIZE ¾ in (1.8–2 cm) long

DIET Larvae are parasitoids on the larvae of solitary mud-nesting wasps; adults feed on nectar

HABITAT Woodlands, grasslands, and deserts

DISTRIBUTION Northern Australia

Giant wood wasp
Rhyssa persuasoria

Found commonly in pine forests, these large wasps drill into tree trunks and logs using their ovipositor and lay their eggs on the larvae of horntails and some beetles. The wasp larvae then feed on their host victims.

SIZE 1½ in (3.6–4 cm) long

DIET Larvae are parasitoids of horntail larvae and some beetles; adult feeding habits are unknown

HABITAT Temperate forests

DISTRIBUTION Northern hemisphere

Female's ovipositor is 1½ in (4 cm) long

Tarantula hawk
Pepsis heros

Tarantula spiders are hunted by this wasp. The female wasp stings and paralyzes a tarantula spider and then drags the spider to its nest. It buries the spider and lays a single egg on the spider's abdomen. After hatching, the larva feeds on the spider.

SIZE 2¾–3¼ in (7–8 cm) long

DIET Tarantulas

HABITAT Tropical and subtropical regions

DISTRIBUTION South America

Mammoth wasp
Scolia procer

The males of this species are much smaller than the females. The females sting larvae of rhinoceros beetles to paralyze them before laying eggs on them. After the wasp larvae hatch, they feed on the beetle larvae.

Hairy hind leg

SIZE 1¾–2¼ in (4.5–5.5 cm)

DIET Larvae are parasitoids on the larvae of rhinoceros beetles; adults feed on nectar

HABITAT Tropical regions

DISTRIBUTION Java, Borneo, and Sumatra

Buff-tailed bumble bee
Bombus terrestris

Bumble bees are social insects that live in small underground nests. A colony consists of worker females, male drones, and an egg-laying queen. Their fur keeps the bumble bees warm, so they can survive in cooler regions.

SIZE   1 in (2.3–2.5 cm) long

DIET   Pollen and nectar

HABITAT   Temperate regions

DISTRIBUTION Worldwide except sub-Saharan Africa and polar regions

Hairy body

Orchid bee
Euglossa asarophora

Special brushlike structures on the hind legs of male orchid bees collect oils and resins from orchids that the bees visit. In an extraordinary courtship ritual, the bees combine these items with special fats in their legs to produce fragrances that attract mates.

SIZE   ½ in (1.2–1.4 cm) long

DIET   Pollen and nectar

HABITAT   Rainforests

DISTRIBUTION   Panama and Costa Rica

Honey bee
Apis mellifera

Originally from Asia, the honey bee is now bred all over the world and people use it for the commercial production of honey. It was first domesticated by the ancient Egyptians more than 4,500 years ago.

SIZE   ½–¾ in (1.2–1.8 cm) long

DIET   Pollen and nectar

HABITAT   Forests, mountains, grasslands, and urban areas

DISTRIBUTION Worldwide except polar regions

Great carpenter bee
Xylocopa latipes

The great carpenter bee is the largest bee in the world. Although huge in size, this bee is quite harmelss. It gets its name from its behavior of making nests in wood. It chews holes in wood with its jaws or deepens burrows made by beetles.

SIZE   1¼–1½ in (3.3–3.6 cm) long

DIET   Pollen and nectar

HABITAT   Woodlands and grasslands

DISTRIBUTION   Southeast Asia

Wool carder bee
Anthidium manicatum

Carding is part of the process of preparing sheep wool for spinning into threads. The wool carder bee is often seen "carding" on mint plants. It scrapes off woolly hairs from the plants, collects a roll of these, and then lines its nest with it.

SIZE ⅜ in (1 cm) long

DIET Pollen and nectar

HABITAT Gardens, meadows, and fields

DISTRIBUTION Europe

Sweat bee
Halictus quadricinctus

Sweat bees pollinate many wildflowers. Their common name comes from the fact that they sometimes feed on the liquid and minerals in the sweat produced by mammals.

SIZE ½–⅝ in (1.3–1.5 cm) long

DIET Pollen, nectar, and sweat of mammals

HABITAT Temperate regions

DISTRIBUTION Southern Europe and the Mediterranean

Plasterer bee
Colletes daviesanus

This bee burrows in soil or in mortar in old brick walls and then covers the walls of its nest cells with a substance that it oozes from its abdomen. Once dry, it turns into a hard lining that waterproofs the nest burrow.

SIZE ½ in (1.1–1.3 cm) long

DIET Pollen and nectar

HABITAT Temperate forests and grasslands

DISTRIBUTION Northern hemisphere

Wood ant
Formica rufa

An aggressive fighter, this ant is capable of spraying a stinging substance called formic acid from its abdomen to ward off an attacker. If a nest is disturbed, the ants swarm out in great numbers to attack the intruder.

SIZE ⅓–½ in (8–10 mm) long

DIET Aphids, flies, caterpillars, beetles, and honeydew

HABITAT Temperate and coniferous forests

DISTRIBUTION Europe and Asia

Wood ants "milk" aphids for food by stroking them until they release drops of sweet honeydew. In return, the ants protect the aphids.

Army ant
Eciton burchellii

Army ants move from place to place. Up to 700,000 ants form a colony, which moves in a narrow column, like an army, through the jungle. Each time they find an area with food, the ants make a temporary nest with their bodies, linking leg to leg from a branch or rock.

SIZE ⅛–½ in (4–12 mm) long

DIET Insects and other arthropods

HABITAT Tropical rainforests

DISTRIBUTION Central and South America

Driver ant
Dorylus nigricans

The predatory driver ants form some of the largest colonies among all social insects—with millions of individual ants. When they emerge from their nests in swarms, animals as large as elephants feel threatened and tend to run away.

SIZE ⅝ in (1.5 cm) long

DIET Insects and small animals

HABITAT Tropical rainforests and savanna

DISTRIBUTION West Africa and Congo

Leaf-cutter ant
Atta laevigata

These ants have strong mandibles (jaws) that they use to cut leaves into tiny pieces. These are then carried back to their vast underground nests. There, they farm a special fungus on chewed pieces of leaves for food.

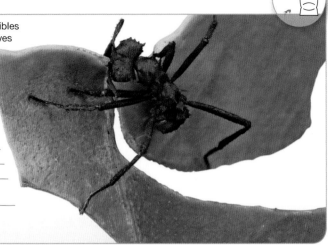

SIZE ⅝ in (1.6 cm) long

DIET Fungus

HABITAT Tropical regions and rainforests

DISTRIBUTION Central and South America

Australian bulldog ant
Myrmecia sp.

Bulldog ants hunt independently. They have large eyes and long, thin mandibles that deliver a powerful bite. Once prey has been caught, it is carried back to the nest for the ant larvae to feed on.

SIZE ¾ in (2.1 cm) long

DIET Honeydew, nectar, seeds, fruits, and small insects

HABITAT Urban areas, forests, woodlands, and heathlands

DISTRIBUTION Australia

The potter wasp brings home live insects for its larvae—its sting

paralyzes

caterpillars, but does not kill them

POTTER WASP
The mason wasp, or potter wasp, builds special nurseries for its larvae using wet mud collected from puddles and the edges of streams. It shapes the clay into nests that look like tiny pots stuck to rocks or tree trunks. Some Native American tribes mold their pottery to look like the wasps' nests.

Arachnids

This class of arthropod includes not just predatory spiders and scorpions, but also scavenging mites and bloodsucking ticks. Arachnids are found worldwide, mostly in a range of habitats on land. Spiders are unique among arachnids for their ability to spin webs of silk, which are used to trap prey. A spiny bellied orb web spider can be seen here, hanging in its web while patiently waiting for a flying insect to get caught.

SCORPION STING
Of the 1,500 species of scorpion, only about 25 have venom that is dangerous to humans. The sting on a scorpion's tail injects the venom.

What are arachnids?

Arachnids come in a diverse range of sizes—from tiny mites that cannot be seen with the naked eye to large, hairy tarantula spiders. Unlike insects, arachnids have just two body segments—the cephalothorax, which is made up of the head and thorax, and the abdomen. Arachnids lack antennae.

First walking leg

Chelicerae

Anatomy

The cephalothorax supports six pairs of structures. The first pair are called chelicerae. These carry the fangs and may be used to inject venom. The next pair may be clawlike in some arachnids and help in feeding. The other four pairs are walking legs. The abdomen of spiders has silk glands, and in scorpions, it extends into a tail.

Cephalothorax

Luring prey

Most arachnids are predatory hunters, but a few lure prey to them. The bolas spider attracts moths by producing a scent similar to the chemicals released by moths during mating. It catches the insects from the air by throwing sticky threads at them as they fly past.

Second walking leg

Long hairs on leg sense air movement

Third walking leg

Mexica red-knee tarantu

Silk from spiders

Spiders produce silk to catch prey, to make cocoons for protecting eggs, or to weave themselves a place to rest. Glands in the abdomen produce the silk and contain a number of tubes called spinnerets that secrete a special liquid. As the spider pulls this out with its hind legs, the liquid thickens into strong, elastic threads of silk.

Defense

If threatened, arachnids often first defend themselves by warning the predator. As a defense tactic, the Sydney funnel-web spider rears up on the ground with its front legs and fangs facing forward to ward off its attacker.

Fourth walking leg

Abdomen has glands that produce silk

Sting on tail

Pedipalp

Half-eaten blowfly

Attacking prey

Some arachnids, such as the northern scorpion, do not spin webs to trap prey. Instead, they hunt by grabbing small insects with their clawlike pedipalps. They only use their venomous sting to overpower larger prey.

Scorpions

All scorpions share two distinct features—a pair of pedipalps (large, clawlike structures near the mouth) and a tail that bears a sting. These creatures hunt at night and usually sense their prey by touch. The 1,500 species of scorpion belong to the order Scorpiones.

Common European scorpion
Buthus occitanus

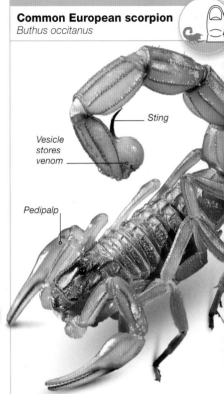

Sting

Vesicle stores venom

Pedipalp

Scorpions can use their venom to poison prey, but they also use it for defense. The venom of the common European scorpion is deadly and can paralyze the heart and lungs of small animals.

SIZE	1¼–1½ in (3–4 cm) long
DIET	Insects
HABITAT	Scrublands
DISTRIBUTION	Northern Africa, the Mediterranean region, and western Asia

Chilean burrowing scorpion
Centromachetes pococki

Most scorpions hide in rock crevices and under loose bark, stones, and logs, but burrowing scorpions make their own shallow burrows in soil up to 2 in (5 cm) deep.

SIZE	4 in (10 cm) long
DIET	Insects
HABITAT	Temperate forests
DISTRIBUTION	South America

Yellow thick-tail scorpion
Androctonus amoreuxi

Yellow thick-tail scorpions are mostly small in size and carry neurotoxins in their venom. These toxins can seriously damage the nervous system of mammals, including humans, and can even cause death.

SIZE 2¾–4 in (7–10 cm) long

DIET Insects

HABITAT Deserts, scrublands

DISTRIBUTION The Sahara and the Middle East

African rock scorpion
Hadogenes troglodytes

A broad, flat abdomen, slender legs, and a thin tail allow rock scorpions to squeeze into slim cracks in rocks, where they spend most of their time hunting or hiding.

SIZE 4–7 in (10–18 cm) long

DIET Other scorpions, spiders, and insects

HABITAT Between cracks in rocks in scrublands

DISTRIBUTION Namibia and South Africa

Imperial scorpion
Pandinus imperator

Sensory hairs cover the tail and pincers of the large imperial scorpion. These detect the vibrations produced by the movement of prey in the air or on the ground, helping the scorpion to find its victims.

SIZE 6–10 in (15–25 cm) long

DIET Lizards, insects, and spiders

HABITAT Tropical forests and savanna

DISTRIBUTION Central and West Africa

A male Imperial scorpion holds the pincers of a female and moves around with her in a "dance" before mating.

SCORPIONS
Most scorpions, including this desert scorpion, carry around 20–50 babies on their backs until the young are old enough to fend for themselves. The young have a soft exoskeleton and are vulnerable. They feed on bits of food left by their mother.

Some desert scorpions warn off predators with a **hissing sound** made by rubbing their sting along the backs of their bodies

Ticks and mites

The order Acari is a diverse group of more than 48,200 species of tick and mite. They are mostly found on land. These arachnids range from scavengers and crop pests to bloodsucking parasites of mammals, birds, and reptiles.

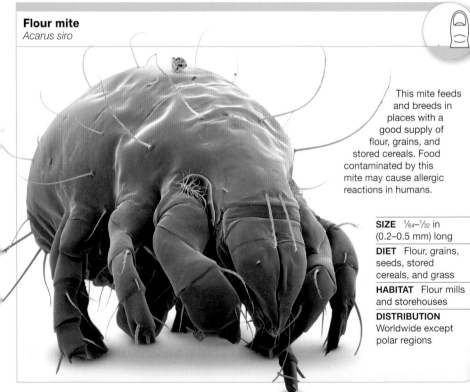

Flour mite
Acarus siro

This mite feeds and breeds in places with a good supply of flour, grains, and stored cereals. Food contaminated by this mite may cause allergic reactions in humans.

SIZE 1/64–1/32 in (0.2–0.5 mm) long

DIET Flour, grains, seeds, stored cereals, and grass

HABITAT Flour mills and storehouses

DISTRIBUTION Worldwide except polar regions

Varroa mite
Varroa cerana

Varroa mites are parasites of both wild and domestic honey bees. Young mites suck out body fluids from bee grubs in the nest. The adult mites hitch rides on the bees and spread to other nests.

SIZE $\frac{1}{16}$ in (1–2 mm) long

DIET Body fluids of bee larvae and adult honey bees

HABITAT On honey bees

DISTRIBUTION Worldwide except polar regions

Common velvet mite
Trombidium holosericeum

These mites are named after the dense, velvetlike "fur" that covers their bodies. They start life as parasites, feeding on other arthropods, but as adults they are predators of insect eggs.

SIZE $\frac{1}{8}$–$\frac{1}{4}$ in (3–5 mm) long

DIET Young mites feed on other arthropods; adults eat insect eggs

HABITAT Temperate regions

DISTRIBUTION Europe and Asia

Lone star tick
Amblyomma americanum

The lone star tick is a parasite of a number of host animals. Its soft, flexible abdomen expands in size to let it feed on a large amount of a host's blood. The tick's saliva can cause redness and irritation on the skin of the host animal and may spread diseases.

Characteristic white spot on body

SIZE $\frac{1}{16}$–$\frac{1}{2}$ in (1–12 mm) long

DIET Blood of mammals and birds

HABITAT Woodlands and scrublands

DISTRIBUTION US and Mexico

Chigger mite
Neotrombicula autumnalis

Chigger mites lay eggs on low-growing plants. After hatching, the larvae climb onto animals passing through the vegetation and attach themselves to a host's skin. The larvae dissolve tiny areas of skin on the host and suck on the nutrients.

SIZE $1/16$ in (2 mm) long

DIET Larvae feed on skin tissues of animals; adults feed on small invertebrates

HABITAT Forest, woodlands, and coastal areas

DISTRIBUTION Worldwide except polar regions

Two-spot spider mite
Tetranychus urticae

The mouthparts of this mite help it to suck up plant sap. After feeding, it leaves pale spots and scars on leaves. It can spread diseases to plants.

SIZE $1/64$ in (0.5 mm) long

DIET Plant sap

HABITAT Temperate regions

DISTRIBUTION Worldwide except polar regions

Red velvet mite
Eutrombidium sp.

Females of this species can lay a batch of up to 4,000 eggs. Newly hatched larvae attach to other insects and suck their body fluids for 1–2 days. Then they drop off and burrow into the soil.

SIZE $1/64$–$1/4$ in (0.5–5 mm) long

DIET Larvae feed on the body fluids of insects; adults feed on insects and insect eggs

HABITAT Scrublands, deciduous forests, and woodlands

DISTRIBUTION Worldwide except polar regions

Mange mite
Sarcoptes scabie

Like the chigger mite, this species feeds on the skin tissues of animals. Adults mate on the body of a host, and the females burrow into the host's skin before laying eggs. This mite causes a disease called mange in dogs.

SIZE $1/64$ in (0.5 mm) long

DIET Larvae feed on the roots of hair; adults feed on skin tissues of animals

HABITAT On the skin or in the roots of hair in mammals

DISTRIBUTION Worldwide except polar regions

Mange mites lack an internal system for breathing and so breathe through their skin.

TRAPS
Some spiders
spin webs to
catch prey, while
others hunt.

▲ The stickiness of the
large webs spun by this
decoy spider helps it to
catch many flying insects.

▲ The net-casting spider
spins a sheet of silk and
holds it between its legs to
trap an approaching insect.

▲ A trapdoor spider digs
a burrow with a lid. Prey
passing on top alerts the
spider, which rushes out
to pull in its victim.

Spiders

More than 42,000 species of these predators
form the order Araneae. Spiders usually
have eight eyes—a few have six—and their
mouthparts (called chelicerae) are tipped
with fangs, which are used to inject venom.

Crablike spiny orb-weaver
Gasteracantha cancriformis

Female orb-weavers spin circular
webs with sticky lines going
from the center outward.
These webs are visited by the
males during courtship, and
they pluck the threads
of the webs to attract
the females.

*Spiny
projections
on abdomen*

SIZE Female
¼–⅓ in (5–9 mm); male
¹⁄₁₆–⅛ in (2–3 mm)

DIET Insects

HABITAT Woodland
edges and shrubs

DISTRIBUTION
Southern US and
the Caribbean

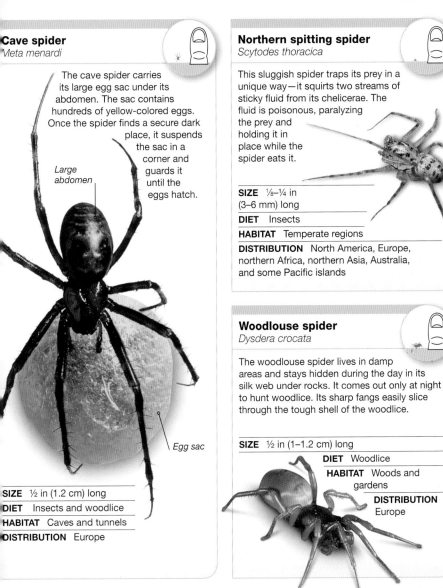

Cave spider
Meta menardi

The cave spider carries its large egg sac under its abdomen. The sac contains hundreds of yellow-colored eggs. Once the spider finds a secure dark place, it suspends the sac in a corner and guards it until the eggs hatch.

Large abdomen

Egg sac

SIZE ½ in (1.2 cm) long

DIET Insects and woodlice

HABITAT Caves and tunnels

DISTRIBUTION Europe

Northern spitting spider
Scytodes thoracica

This sluggish spider traps its prey in a unique way—it squirts two streams of sticky fluid from its chelicerae. The fluid is poisonous, paralyzing the prey and holding it in place while the spider eats it.

SIZE ⅛–¼ in (3–6 mm) long

DIET Insects

HABITAT Temperate regions

DISTRIBUTION North America, Europe, northern Africa, northern Asia, Australia, and some Pacific islands

Woodlouse spider
Dysdera crocata

The woodlouse spider lives in damp areas and stays hidden during the day in its silk web under rocks. It comes out only at night to hunt woodlice. Its sharp fangs easily slice through the tough shell of the woodlice.

SIZE ½ in (1–1.2 cm) long

DIET Woodlice

HABITAT Woods and gardens

DISTRIBUTION Europe

Daddy long-legs spider
Pholcus phalangioides

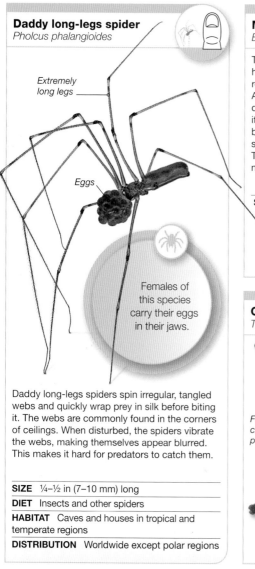

Extremely long legs

Eggs

Females of this species carry their eggs in their jaws.

Daddy long-legs spiders spin irregular, tangled webs and quickly wrap prey in silk before biting it. The webs are commonly found in the corners of ceilings. When disturbed, the spiders vibrate the webs, making themselves appear blurred. This makes it hard for predators to catch them.

SIZE	¼–½ in (7–10 mm) long
DIET	Insects and other spiders
HABITAT	Caves and houses in tropical and temperate regions
DISTRIBUTION	Worldwide except polar regions

Mexican red-kneed tarantula
Brachypelma smithi

This large, hairy spider can hunt small mammals and reptiles. Like many tropical American tarantulas, it defends itself by rubbing its hind legs against its body. This releases barbed, stinging hairs from its body. These hairs irritate the eyes, nose, and mouth of a predator.

SIZE	2–3 in (5–7.5 cm) long
DIET	Large insects
HABITAT	Tropical deciduous forests
DISTRIBUTION	Mexico

Goliath tarantula
Theraphosa blondi

Fang-bearing chelicerae point forward

Hairs on legs are sensitive to air movements and help the spider to sense prey

Northern widow spider
Latrodectus mactans

Although small in size, this spider is very venomous. Its venom affects the nervous system of its victims, paralyzing them. Its bite is very painful, but rarely fatal to humans.

SIZE ⅛–½ in (4–13 mm) long

DIET Insects and other invertebrates

HABITAT Grasslands

DISTRIBUTION North America

The Goliath tarantula is one of the largest spiders on Earth. It lives in burrows and can sense vibrations on the ground, which helps it to detect prey. It fends off predators with stinging hairs released from its body. Adult females often surround their eggs with these hairs as a way of protecting them from attackers.

SIZE 4¾–5½ in (12–14 cm) long

DIET Insects, lizards, frogs, and small mammals

HABITAT Rainforests

DISTRIBUTION South America

European wolf spider
Pardosa amentata

Wolf spiders do not spin webs but instead hunt prey on the ground. They stalk prey patiently before jumping on their victims with a burst of speed.

SIZE ¼–⅓ in (5–8 mm) long

DIET Insects

HABITAT Woodlands, grasslands, and gardens

DISTRIBUTION Europe

Goldenrod crab spider
Misumena vatia

Females of this species can change their color from white to yellow to disguise themselves among the flowers on which they rest. Insects visiting these flowers fail to notice the camouflaged spiders and end up as food for them.

SIZE ⅛–½ in (3–11 mm) long

DIET
Nectar-feeding insects

HABITAT Grasslands, woodlands, and gardens

DISTRIBUTION
North America and Europe

Brown jumping spider
Evarcha arcuata

Jumping spiders have excellent eyesight. Their eight eyes allow them to sense movement from any direction to avoid predators. Their large, forward-facing eyes also allow them to judge distance accurately to pounce on prey. Before leaping, a jumping spider produces a safety line of silk just in case it misses its target.

SIZE ⅛–¼ in (5–7 mm) long

DIET Insects and other spiders

HABITAT Grasslands

DISTRIBUTION Europe and Asia

Grass crab spider
Tibellus oblongus

This spider is found among tall, dry grasses. It lies with its legs outstretched along the length of a blade of grass while waiting to ambush prey.

Elegant jumping spider
Chrysilla lauta

This jumping spider often attacks ants—it pounces on its victim and bites it, injecting venom, but then retreats and waits. It repeats this process and moves in to feed only when the ant is paralyzed.

SIZE	⅛–⅓ in (3–9 mm) long
DIET	Ants
HABITAT	Rainforests
DISTRIBUTION	Eastern Asia

Brightly colored body

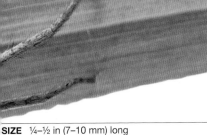

SIZE	¼–½ in (7–10 mm) long
DIET	Insects
HABITAT	Meadows, gardens, and coastal areas
DISTRIBUTION	Northern hemisphere

Bites from the tarantula spider were believed to be poisonous in 16th-century Taranto, Italy, and the remedy involved a form of

wild dancing

called the tarantella

TARANTULA
A large, hairy South American tarantula may look venomous, but it is actually harmless to humans. When threatened, a tarantula will first rear up on its hind legs and raise its fangs in an aggressive posture to scare off its attacker.

Sun-spiders and pseudoscorpions

Sun-spiders belong to the order Solifugae and number around 1,10 species. The unrelated scorpion-shaped pseudoscorpions form the order Pseudoscorpiones, which consists of about 3,300 species.

American sun-spider
Eremobates durangonus

Although found commonly in deserts, this arachnid tends to hide from sunlight. It prefers to stay in shaded corners, only coming out at night to hunt. It lacks venom and kills prey with its large mandibles (jaws).

SIZE   1–1¼ in (2.5–3 cm) long

DIET   Insects and other small animals

HABITAT   Deserts and mountains

DISTRIBUTION   Parts of northern and Central America

Segmented abdomen

Small eyes

Large jaws

Maritime pseudoscorpion
Neobisium maritimum

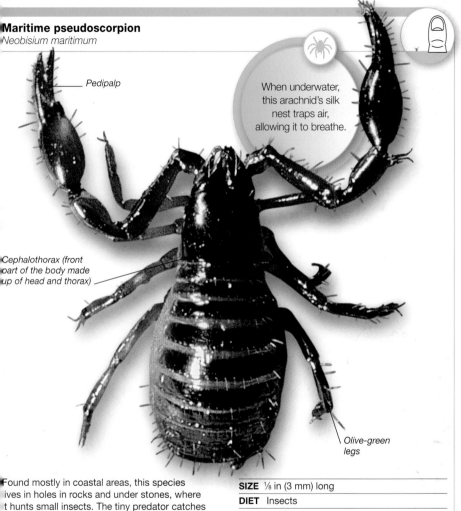

Pedipalp

When underwater, this arachnid's silk nest traps air, allowing it to breathe.

Cephalothorax (front part of the body made up of head and thorax)

Olive-green legs

Found mostly in coastal areas, this species lives in holes in rocks and under stones, where it hunts small insects. The tiny predator catches small prey with its pedipalps and releases a venom to paralyze its victims, before shredding them to pieces with its chelicerae.

SIZE	⅛ in (3 mm) long
DIET	Insects
HABITAT	Coastal regions
DISTRIBUTION	Europe

Other arachnids

The lesser-known relatives of spiders and scorpions include the whip-scorpions, whip-spiders, and harvestmen. Whip-scorpions form the order Thelyphonida, which includes about 100 species. Whip-spiders form the order Amblypygi and number around 160 species. About 6,125 species of harvestman make up the order Opiliones.

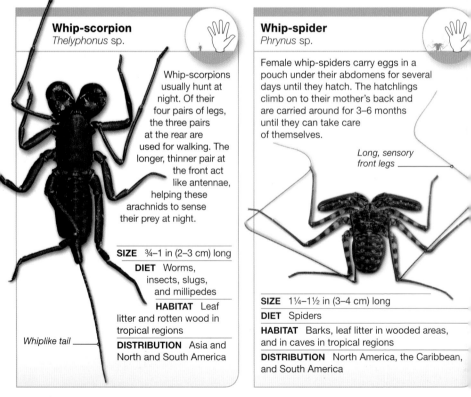

Whip-scorpion
Thelyphonus sp.

Whip-scorpions usually hunt at night. Of their four pairs of legs, the three pairs at the rear are used for walking. The longer, thinner pair at the front act like antennae, helping these arachnids to sense their prey at night.

Whiplike tail

SIZE ¾–1 in (2–3 cm) long

DIET Worms, insects, slugs, and millipedes

HABITAT Leaf litter and rotten wood in tropical regions

DISTRIBUTION Asia and North and South America

Whip-spider
Phrynus sp.

Female whip-spiders carry eggs in a pouch under their abdomens for several days until they hatch. The hatchlings climb on to their mother's back and are carried around for 3–6 months until they can take care of themselves.

Long, sensory front legs

SIZE 1¼–1½ in (3–4 cm) long

DIET Spiders

HABITAT Barks, leaf litter in wooded areas, and in caves in tropical regions

DISTRIBUTION North America, the Caribbean, and South America

Horned harvestman
Phalangium opilio

Like other harvestmen, the eyes of this species are located close together on a "turret" above the body. The eyes are simple and cannot see well, but help these arachnids to sense light from their surroundings for moving around.

Second pair of legs is very long

When attacked, the horned harvestman detaches its legs, which continue to twitch, confusing its predator.

SIZE ⅛–⅓ in (4–9 mm) long

DIET Aphids, caterpillars, leafhoppers, and decaying organic matter

HABITAT Woods, meadows, and gardens

DISTRIBUTION Native in Europe and Asia; introduced in North America, northern Africa, and New Zealand

Say's harvestman
Vonones sayi

This harvestman defends itself in an unusual way. When threatened or disturbed, it produces a fluid from its mouth, which mixes with toxic secretions from special abdominal glands. It then uses its long legs to smear this toxic mixture on its attacker, warding it off.

Small pedipalps

SIZE ½–⅝ in (1–1.5 cm) long

DIET Insects

HABITAT Under stones and logs in tropical regions

DISTRIBUTION North and Central America

Other arthropods

Aside from insects and arachnids, arthropods also include smaller groups of invertebrates, such as crustaceans, myriapods, and non-insect hexapods. Most crustaceans live in water, but a few live only on land. The tiny non-insect hexapods and the multilegged myriapods crawl around in moist leaf litter on forest floors. On the left is a myriapod called the giant red millipede. Tiny hooked claws on its feet help it to grip the ground while moving, as well as to climb trees.

MOLTING
Like most arthropods, water springtails mature by shedding their exoskeleton at regular intervals.

Myriapods, crustaceans, and non-insect hexapods

The wingless non-insect hexapods move around on six legs, while the wormlike myriapods—including centipedes and millipedes—run along on many legs. Myriapods have a hard exoskeleton like the crustaceans, but it is not waterproof, which means these bugs need to stay in damp surroundings.

As a **defensive tactic**, millipedes coil up into a tight ball when disturbed.

Myriapods

A myriapod's body is divided into a head and trunk, and there is no separate thorax or abdomen. Centipedes have a single pair of legs on each trunk segment, which they wiggle rapidly to move. Millipedes have two pairs of legs per segment, which they move in a gliding, wavelike sequence to push themselves forward.

Trunk is divided into many segments

Millipede

Bright red leg

Domed
exoskeleton

Woodlouse

Crustaceans

The hard exoskeletons of arthropods are made of a substance called chitin, but in crustaceans it is made stronger by a mineral called calcium carbonate. The body of the woodlouse, one of the few crustaceans to live on land, is divided into 14 segments.

Each **trunk segment** has two pairs of legs

Head has mandibles and one pair of antennae

Exoskeleton protects body parts

NON-INSECT HEXAPODS

Hexapods (which means "six-footed") include not only insects but also three other groups—springtails, proturans, and diplurans—known collectively as non-insect hexapods.

Insects have eyes and antennae that allow them to see and sense their surroundings. Many have wings. Insects have clearly visible mouthparts.

Honey bee

Non-insect hexapods lack wings, and some do not even have eyes or antennae. Their mouthparts are hidden in a pouch below the head.

Water springtail

Myriapods

This group of land-living arthropods includes centipedes, millipedes, and other related species. About 3,000 species of centipede make up the class Chilopoda and all can run fast. The slow-moving millipedes of the class Diplopoda number around 10,000 species.

▲ The mouthparts of black millipedes are short and stout, for nibbling plants, roots, and decaying wood.

▲ Giant desert centipedes hunt lizards, frogs, and insects. They kill prey with their venomous claws.

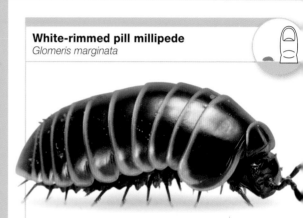

White-rimmed pill millipede
Glomeris marginata

Millipedes have between 36 and 450 legs, two pairs growing from each body segment. Pill millipedes are a short, squat species with only 11–13 body segments. Like all pill millipedes, this one rolls itself into a ball when attacked by a bird or ants. It looks quite similar to a pill woodlouse.

SIZE	¼–¾ in (0.6–2 cm) long
DIET	Decaying leaves
HABITAT	Soil and leaf litter in broad-leaved forests
DISTRIBUTION	Europe, parts of Asia, and Northern Africa

Tanzanian flat-backed millipede
Coromus diaphorus

Flat-backed millipedes are less rounded than other millipedes and can be mistaken for centipedes, which are usually flat in shape. The tough flattened body of this millipede allows it to squeeze under logs and stones to hide in the leaf litter of the forests in which it lives.

Shiny body is covered in grooves —

SIZE 1½–2½ in (4–6 cm) long

DIET Dead leaves, other decaying plant matter, roots, and fruit

HABITAT Tropical forests

DISTRIBUTION Africa

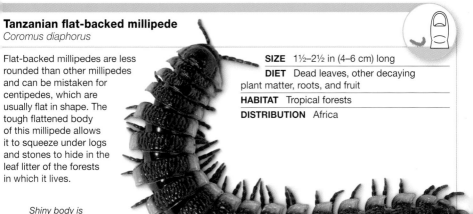

African giant millipede
Archispirostreptus gigas

The African giant millipede is the largest of all millipedes. This species defends itself from predators in two ways. It can curl up into a spiral ball exposing only its hard exoskeleton, which makes it difficult for predators to bite it. It can also ooze a toxic fluid from its body to deter predators.

SIZE 8–11 in (20–28 cm) long

DIET Decaying organic matter

HABITAT Tropical forests

DISTRIBUTION Africa

Tiger giant centipede
Scolopendra hardwickei

Claw

This centipede gets its name from the tigerlike markings on its body and its predatory nature. It hunts at night and can overpower and catch prey larger than itself, including mice. The centipede attacks prey with the claws on its first trunk segment, which carry venom.

Bright colors on its body warn off predators

SIZE 8–10 in (20–25 cm) long

DIET Large insects and small mammals

HABITAT Under rotting wood, loose bark, and leaf litter in rainforests and grasslands

DISTRIBUTION Southeast Asia

Banded stone centipede
Lithobius variegatus

Commonly found near deciduous trees, this species has strong limbs, which help it to climb trees in search of food. A flattened body allows the predator to hunt in tight spaces for small insects and woodlice. In summer, it sticks to feeding in leaf litter, limiting its movement in order to conserve body moisture.

SIZE ¾–1¼ in (2–3 cm) long

DIET Small arthropods, such as woodlice and millipedes

HABITAT In leaf litter and on trees in temperate, tropical, and coniferous forests

DISTRIBUTION Europe

Yellow earth centipede
Geophilus flavus

Soil centipedes are a family of centipede that live in the soil and under rocks. The short legs and rectangular head of this centipede allow it to move quickly through soil and leaf litter.

SIZE ¾–1½ in (2–3.5 cm) long

DIET Small, soil-dwelling invertebrates

HABITAT Soil in forests and coastal areas

DISTRIBUTION Europe, Australia, and North and South America

Brown stone centipede
Lithobius forficatus

Unlike many millipedes that roll into a ball when threatened, the brown stone centipede runs away quickly. It is mostly found in the upper layers of soil, particularly under rotting logs.

SIZE ¾–1¼ in (2–3 cm)

DIET Woodlice, spiders, mites, and insects

HABITAT Forests, gardens, and coastal areas

DISTRIBUTION Worldwide except polar regions

House centipede
Scutigera coleoptrata

The antennae of this centipede are very sensitive to smell and touch, allowing it to sense prey even in complete darkness. Once it finds prey, it pounces with its legs, stinging them with its powerful venom.

SIZE 1–2 in (2.5–5 cm) long

DIET Spiders, bedbugs, termites, cockroaches, silverfish, ants, and other insects

HABITAT Caves and houses

DISTRIBUTION Worldwide except polar regions

The house centipede's long antennae resemble its hind legs, making it difficult to make out its head.

As they grow, millipedes
shed their exoskeleton
regularly and

eat it

for extra energy

MADAGASCAN FIRE MILLIPEDE
The vibrant colors on the body of this millipede warn predators that it may be poisonous. If a predator continues to threaten it, it rolls up into a ball and oozes out toxic chemicals that may burn the predator's skin.

Non-insect hexapods

Three small groups of arthropods—springtails, proturans, and diplurans—are known as non-insect hexapods. The class Collembola includes about 8,100 species of springtail, the class Protura has about 750 species of proturan, and the class Diplura contains around 1,000 species of dipluran.

Water springtail
Podura aquatica

This water-dwelling species is often found on the surfaces of ponds and puddles. It has a long, fork-shaped organ called a furcula attached to the underside of its abdomen. It releases its furcula like a spring to jump around.

SIZE Up to 3/16 in (2 mm) long

DIET Decaying organic matter

HABITAT Freshwater ditches, puddles, ponds, canals, and bogs

DISTRIBUTION Northern hemisphere

When many water springtails gather together in ponds and streams, they can turn the surface of the water dark.

Pale springtail
Onychiurus sp.

Unlike the water springtail, these species lack a furcula and are unable to jump away from predators. Most pale springtails also lack eyes and sense their environment with a pair of antennae instead.

SIZE ³⁄₁₆–¹⁄₃ in (2–9 mm) long

DIET Plants, decaying organic matter, and fungi

HABITAT In soil and leaf litter in scrublands, woodlands, and mountains

DISTRIBUTION Worldwide

Barred springtail
Entomobrya sp.

These springtails graze on algae and lichen on tree trunks, rocks, buildings, and cliffs. They can feed in these exposed places because they are more resistant to water loss than most other springtails.

SIZE ¹⁄₁₆–¹⁄₃ in (1–8 mm) long

DIET Algae and lichen

HABITAT Tree barks, rocks, and buildings

DISTRIBUTION Worldwide except polar regions

European proturan
Eosentomon delicatum

Proturans live in soil and leaf litter. They lack body pigment (coloring), eyes, and antennae. They use their front legs as sensory feelers, and walk using their middle and hind legs.

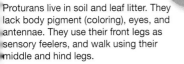

SIZE ¹⁄₆₄–¹⁄₈ in (0.5–2 mm) long

DIET Decaying organic matter and fungi

HABITAT In soil and leaf litter in forests and woodlands

DISTRIBUTION Europe

Long-tailed dipluran
Campodea fragilis

The dipluran is blind and has a long body and antennae. It uses its long pair of flexible, tail-like structures called cerci like a second pair of antennae.

SIZE ¹⁄₈–¹⁄₄ in (3–6 mm) long

DIET Decaying organic matter and fungi

HABITAT Soil and leaf litter

DISTRIBUTION Worldwide except polar regions

Crustaceans

Most crustaceans live in the sea, some live in freshwater, but a few, such as woodlice, live only on land. There are about 3,000 different species of woodlouse, which form part of the order Isopoda.

Black-headed woodlouse
Porcellio spinicornis

This woodlouse can easily be identified by its black head and the row of yellow blotches on either side of its body. Like all woodlice, it does not produce urine and instead releases smelly ammonia gas as waste.

SIZE 4–4¾ in (10–12 cm) long

DIET Decaying organic matter

HABITAT Tropical forests, woodlands, and grasslands

DISTRIBUTION Europe and North America

Common pill woodlouse
Armadillidium vulgare

The segmented body covering of this woodlouse works like a shell to protect it. When threatened, the common pill woodlouse rolls itself into a hard and tight ball, which protects its softer body parts from predators.

SIZE ½–¾ in (1–1.8 cm) long

DIET Decaying organic matter, algae, and lichen

HABITAT Calcium-rich soils in forests and coastal areas

DISTRIBUTION Eurasia and North America

Common shiny woodlouse
Oniscus asellus

The common shiny woodlouse has a gray body with irregular yellow patches, which store calcium. The woodlice living in calcium-poor soils will eat the shed exoskeleton after molting. This recycles the calcium, which strengthens their body covering.

SIZE ½ in–¾ in (10–16 mm) long

DIET Decaying organic matter

HABITAT In leaf litter and under logs in temperate woods and gardens

DISTRIBUTION Europe and North and South America

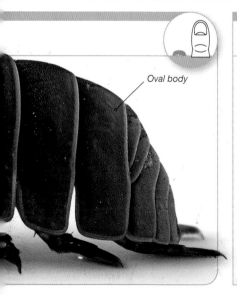

Oval body

Ant woodlouse
Platyarthrus hoffmannseggi

Ant woodlice have a close relationship to ants, which is beneficial to both insects. The woodlice live in the nests of ants and feed on ant droppings. They also help to keep the nests clean, which is of benefit to the ants.

SIZE Up to ⅛ in (4 mm) long

DIET Ant droppings

HABITAT Ant nests in woods and gardens

DISTRIBUTION Europe, North Africa, the Middle East, and North America

Record breakers

BIGGEST BUGS

★ **Chan's megastick** (*Phobaeticus chani*) is the world's longest stick insect. It can grow up to 22½ in (56.7 cm) long, including its legs. Not including its legs, it can be 14 in (35.7 cm) long, which means it is also the insect with the longest body.

★ **Queen Alexandra's birdwing** (*Ornithoptera alexandrae*) is the world's largest butterfly and has the longest wingspan of any insect, measuring up to 12 in (30 cm) from the outer edge of one wing to the other.

★ The **Atlas moth** (*Attacus atlas*) is the largest moth in the world—its wings cover an area of 62 sq in (400 sq cm).

★ The **giant African millipede** (*Archispirostreptus gigas*) is the longest millipede in the world, reaching lengths of up to 11 in (28 cm).

★ The longest beetle in the world is the **Hercules beetle** (*Dynastes hercules*) found in Central America. It can measure up to 7½ in (19 cm) in length.

STRONGEST BUGS

❶ The **orbatid mite** (*Archegozetes longisetosus*) is a tiny, soil-dwelling mite; it can carry 1,180 times its own weight—equal to a human being lifting 80 tons (73 metric tons).

❷ A **horned dung beetle** (*Onthophagus Taurus*) can pull 1,141 times its own body weight. This is equal to a man lifting two fully loaded 18-wheel trucks.

❸ A **leafcutter ant** (*Atta laevigata*) can carry leaves weighing up to 50 times its body weight.

LONGEST JUMPS

❶ A **cat flea** (*Ctenocephalides felis*) can jump a distance up to 150 times its body length.

❷ The **froghopper** (*Philaenus spumarius*) is 60 times heavier than a cat flea, but can jump a distance 70 times its own body length.

❸ **Jumping spiders** can jump over a distance of about 14 in (35 cm). They use their rear legs to spring toward their prey.

LONGEST LIFESPANS

A North American cicada called *Magicicada septendecim* lives underground for 17 years as a nymph, and just a few hours or days as an adult.

A **honeypot ant queen** of the *Myrmecocystus* genus was found to have lived for 11 years.

Two larvae of the **golden jewel beetle** (*Buprestis aurulenta*) found in timbers in a Canadian building were 51 years old.

The average lifespan of a butterfly is 3–6 weeks, but the **monarch butterfly** (*Danaus plexippus*) can live for up to a year.

LARGEST GROUPS

❶ **Lake flies** (*Chaoborus edulis* Edward), found commonly over Lake Victoria in central Africa, form swarms containing trillions of flies. These hover over the lake and the surrounding villages as dark clouds.

❷ **Desert locusts** (*Schistocerca gregaria*) form incredibly large swarms, which may contain as many as 10 billion individuals.

❸ **Leafcutter ants** (*Atta cephalotes*) form some of the largest colonies in the insect world, with up to 8 million individuals in each nest.

"Cakes" made of lake flies are eaten by villagers living around Lake Victoria. They are very rich in protein.

HEAVIEST BUGS

The **Goliath bird-eating spider** (*Therophosa blondi*) is the heaviest species of spider and can weigh more than 5 oz (150 g).

A grub of the **Goliath beetle** (*Goliathus giganteus*) can weigh up to 3.5 oz (100 g) when fully grown. It is the heaviest known beetle grub.

The **giant weta** (*Deinacrida heteracantha*), a type of cricket, weighs in at 2.5 oz (71 g).

LONGEST MIGRATIONS

❶ **Monarch butterflies** (*Danaus plexippus*) undertake the biggest insect migration, when 250 million of them fly nearly 3,100 miles (5,000 km) from Canada to Mexico to spend the winter in warm sheltered valleys amid Mexico's pine-covered mountains.

❷ Each year, **dragonflies** migrate from India to the Maldives, Seychelles, and finally East Africa, covering a distance of 2,175 miles (3,500 km).

Incredible bugs

AMAZING NUMBERS

★ About **1 million species of insect** had been identified globally by early 2012.

★ About **80 percent** of known insects undergo complete metamorphosis.

★ Beetles form the biggest insect order with about **350,000 species**, which make up **35 percent** of all insects.

★ The nests of some social insects contain millions of members. A termite nest in South America was found to contain about **3 million individuals**.

★ Some termite queens in East Africa can lay one egg every two seconds, which adds up to **43,200 eggs each day**.

★ Although spiders look creepy, only **30–40** of the 50,000 known species are dangerous to humans.

★ Jumping spiders make up the largest family of spiders in the world (Salticidae), which has about **4,400 known species**.

HARMFUL BUGS

• **Female Anopheles mosquitoes** carry the parasite that causes malaria. The disease kills around 665,000 people every year.

• Of all sting-bearing hornets, the **giant Japanese hornet** delivers the greatest amount of venom in a single sting. It is the most dangerous animal in Japan, killing more than 40 people each year.

• **Driver ants** set out in search of food in their millions and can consume almost every animal in their way.

• The sting of the **fire ant** carries a venom containing a substance called piperidine. This produces an intense burning sensation on human skin.

• The **deathstalker scorpion** is the most venomous scorpion on Earth, but the mixture of toxins in its venom is usually only dangerous to small children, the elderly, or sick people.

• The **Brazilian huntsman** is the most poisonous spider the world. Only 0.00000021 oz (0.006 mg) of its venom is needed to kill a mouse.

The jaws of driver ants are so strong that some tribes in East Africa use the jaws for stitching wounds.

PRODUCTS FROM INSECTS

Honey

Honey bees are bred in captivity to produce honey. Beekeepers collect surplus honey from honeycombs and sell it.

In 2011, about 200,000 tons (180,000 metric tons) of honey was consumed in the US.

Beeswax

Wax produced by young worker honey bees is commonly used to make candles, varnishes, and food preservatives.

Royal jelly

This is made from a fluid secreted by worker honey bees and is believed to have medicinal properties.

Food for humans

Humans eat about 500 species of insect. Stir-fried crickets are a delicacy some nations.

◆ Silk

This shiny fabric is woven from the threads of silk moth cocoons.

◆ Lac

Some scale insects produce a resinous secretion called lac, which is used to dye wool, as a violin varnish, and as a medicinal drug.

◆ Ink

The galls (swellings on leaves) produced by the oak wasp contain tannins, a major ingredient of iron gall ink, which was widely used by writers from the Middle Ages to the 19th century because of its waterproof nature.

◆ Jewelry

The brightly colored wings of butterflies and hard elytra (wing cases) of beetles are made into brooches and pendants.

STUDYING BUGS

Many different scientists study the various orders and families of bugs. Some common fields of study are listed here.

- **Entomology**—all insects

- **Apiology**—bees

- **Dipterology**—flies

- **Colepterology**—beetles

- **Myrmecology**—ants

- **Acarology**—ticks and mites

- **Arachnology**—spiders, scorpions, and related species

- **Parasitology**—parasites

Glossary

Antennae A pair of sensory organs on the heads of some invertebrates, such as insects, used to detect vibrations, smells, and tastes.

Appendage A limb or other sensory organ, such as an antenna, on the body of an insect.

Aquatic Living or growing in or near water.

Arthropod An invertebrate with an exoskeleton, a segmented body, and jointed legs.

Asexual reproduction A form of reproduction in which an animal produces offspring without mating with another animal.

Brackish Water that is partly salty and partly fresh. Brackish water is found in coastal swamps and river mouths, where fresh water mixes with seawater.

Brood cell A tiny space in the nest of a bee or wasp where a single egg is laid.

Bug An informal term for many land-dwelling arthropods.

Camouflage Colors or patterns on an animal's body that allow it to blend with its surroundings.

Caterpillar The wingless larva of a butterfly or moth. It has legs and powerful jaws.

Cellulose A complex sugar found in plants.

Cephalothorax The front part of the body of an arachnid, which is made up of the head and thorax.

Cerci A pair of long tail-like structures on the abdomen of some insects.

Chelicerae The first pair of structures on an arachnid's cephalothorax, nearest to its mouth. They may carry fangs or teeth at the tips, which arachnids, such as spiders, use to inject venom.

Chrysalis The hard case of a butterfly pupa.

Class A large group that contains many closely related orders of animals.

Cocoon A silk case made by larvae of many insects in which they pupate.

Colony A group of animals of a species that live together.

Compound eye An eye made up of many smaller units, each of which can receive light and "see." Arthropods have compound eyes.

Coniferous Describes trees, including pine and fir, that lack flowers and fruits and produce cones containing their seeds.

Courtship Behavior that helps to form a bond between a male and a female before mating.

Deciduous Describes trees that shed leaves in the fall and grow new ones in spring.

Elytra The forewings of some insects that fit like a protective case over the thin hind wings.

Endangered species A species that is in danger of becoming extinct, such as the Queen Alexandra's birdwing butterfly.

Exoskeleton A hard, outer skeleton that surrounds an arthropod's body and gives it shape and protection.

Family A group that contains closely related genera (singular, **genus**) of animals.

Gall Hard, lumpy growth of plant tissue, triggered by chemicals from some insects, such as wasps.

Genus A group that contains closely related species of animals.

Habitat The environment in which an animal lives.

Haltere In two-winged flies, a small pin-shaped organ that takes the place of hind wings. Halteres help flies to balance themselves in flight.

Honeydew A sweet substance produced by plant-sucking aphids.

Host An animal on which a parasite feeds.

Invertebrate Any animal without a backbone.

Larva The immature, often wormlike, form that hatches from the eggs of many insects and other invertebrates.

Life cycle The stages that an animal goes through from birth to death.

Maggot Legless larva of flies and other insects.

Mammal A vertebrate that has hair or fur and feeds its young on milk.

Mandibles A pair of jaws that many arthropods use to bite, cut, or carry food.

Metamorphosis A major change in an animal's body shape during its

...fe cycle. Caterpillars turn into butterflies or moths through metamorphosis.

Migration A journey undertaken by an animal due to seasonal changes, usually to find food or to breed.

Mimic To resemble something, such as a leaf or another animal. This helps in camouflage.

Molting Shedding of the exoskeleton by an arthropod after regular periods of time that allows its body to grow.

Nectar A sugary liquid produced by flowers on which many insects feed.

Nervous system A system in an animal's body that is mainly made up of fibers called nerves, which send and receive signals to and from various body parts.

Nocturnal An animal that is active at night.

Nymph An early stage of development of an invertebrate that generally looks and lives in the same way as the animal's adult form.

Ocelli Simple eyes that only sense the level of light.

Order A large group that contains closely related families of animals.

Organism A life-form, such as a plant, fungus, or animal.

Ovipositor A tubelike organ in the females of some animals, used for laying eggs.

Ovoviviparous Producing eggs that hatch inside the mother's body.

Parasite An animal that lives on, or inside, the body of another species, known as the host. It feeds on and harms the host, but does not kill it.

Parasitoid An animal that grows by feeding on a living host and eventually kills it.

Pedipalps The second pair of structures on the cephalothorax of some arachnids. They may be clawlike.

Pheromones Chemicals released by an animal to attract a member of the opposite sex of the same species.

Pigment A substance that colors the tissues of an invertebrate.

Pollination Transfer of pollen from one flower to another for reproduction. Some flowers are pollinated by the wind, but in most cases, insects act as pollen carriers.

Predator An animal that hunts, kills, and eats other animals.

Prey An animal that is hunted, killed, and eaten by a predator.

Proboscis Straw-shaped mouthparts of insects, such as butterflies, that are used for sucking food.

Pupa The stage in the life cycle of certain insects in which the larva stays protected within a special case as it transforms into an adult.

Rainforests Dense tropical forests that receive heavy rainfall.

Rostrum Slender, beak-shaped mouthparts that some insects use to pierce and suck up food.

Savanna Grassland with widely spaced trees found in hot regions of the world, such as Africa.

Scavenger An animal that feeds on the dead remains of others.

Species A group of animals that breed only with each other.

Spiracle A tiny breathing hole on the body surface of many arthropods.

Temperate Relating to the region of the world between the tropical and polar regions that is neither too hot nor too cold.

Terrestrial Living only on land.

Territory An area defended by an animal from others of its own species.

Thorax The middle part of an arthropod's body, between the head and abdomen. It bears the wings and legs.

Tropical Relating to the hot region of the world spanning the equator. It is a broad band around the middle part of the globe.

Tubers Short, fleshy underground stems or roots of plants such as potato.

Tundra A vast, frozen, treeless region lying north of the Arctic Circle.

Vertebrate Any animal with a backbone.

Wetlands An area of land that remains flooded with water for most part of the year, and so the soil is permanently wet.

Wingspan The measurement from the tip of one wing of a flying insect to that of the other when the wings are outstretched.

Index

Acknowledgments

Dorling Kindersley would like to thank: Caitlin Doyle for proofreading; Helen Peters for indexing and Claire Bowers, Fabian Harry, and Romaine Werblow for DK Picture Library assistance.

The publishers would also like to thank the following for their kind permission to reproduce their photographs:

(Key: a-above; b-below/bottom; c-center; f-far; l-left; r-right; t-top)

2–3 Igor Siwanowicz: (c). 4 Corbis: Joe McDonald (cl). 5 Corbis: Piotr Naskrecki / Minden Pictures (tr, br). PunchStock: Westend61 (bl). 6 Corbis: Oswald Eckstein. 7 Corbis: Fred Bavendam / Minden Pictures (br). 8 Alamy Images: D. Hurst (tc). 9 Corbis: Nigel Cattlin / Visuals Unlimited (bc). 10 Dorling Kindersley: Oxford Scientific Films (tr). FLPA: Richard Becker (bl). 11 Alamy Images: blickwinkel (bl). Corbis: Mark Moffett / Minden Pictures (cr). FLPA: Michael & Patricia Fogden / Minden Pictures (bc). Getty Images: Paul Souders / The Image Bank (tr). 12 Alamy Images: blickwinkel / Hecker (tc). Corbis: Pete Oxford / Minden Pictures (br); Cyril Ruoso / JH Editorial / Minden Pictures (c). Getty Images: Colin Milkins / Oxford Scientific (cl). 13 Corbis: Frans Lanting (bc); Solvin Zankl / Visuals Unlimited (tl). FLPA: Chien Lee / Minden Pictures (cr). 14 Dorling Kindersley: Natural History Museum, London (tr, cr). 15 Corbis: Visuals Unlimited (tl). Dorling Kindersley: Natural History Museum, London (cr). FLPA: Mark Moffett / Minden Pictures (br). Getty Images: Kjell Sandved, Butterfly Alphabet, Inc. / Oxford Scientific (tc); Stefano Stefani / Photodisc (c). 16–17 Corbis: Mark Moffett / Minden Pictures. 18 Corbis: Alex Wild / Visuals Unlimited. 19 Getty Images: Densey Clyne / Oxford Scientific (bc). 21 Corbis: Alex Wild / Visuals Unlimited (tr). 22 FLPA: Albert Lleal / Minden Pictures (br). 23 Alamy Images: Ray Wilson (tl). FLPA: Albert Lleal / Minden Pictures (tr); Steve Trewhella (b). 24 Dorling Kindersley: Natural History Museum, London (bc). 25 Alamy Images: Premaphotos (tr); WILDLIFE GmbH (br). Photoshot: Gerry Cambridge / NHPA (bl). 26 Dorling Kindersley: Photo Biopix.dk (bl). 27 Dorling Kindersley: Forrest L. Mitchell / James Laswel (bl). Getty Images: Altrendo Nature (tr); Marcos Veiga / age fotostock (tl). 28 Dorling Kindersley: Forrest L. Mitchell / James Laswe (tl). 28–29 Getty Images: Shem Compion / Gallo Images (c). 29 Dorling Kindersley: Forrest L. Mitchell / James Laswel (clb). 34–35 Photoshot: J.C. Carton. 36–37 Alamy Images: blickwinkel / Schuetz (c). 37 Alamy Images: A & J Visage (br). 39 Corbis: DLILLC (tl). Getty Images: Ar* Wolfe / Stone (tr). 41 Corbis: Hugo Willocx / Foto Natura / Minden Pictures (cr). Dorling Kindersley: Natural History Museum, London (bl). Martin Heigan: (tr). 42 Alamy Images: Nigel Cattlin (tl); Premaphotos (cl, bl). 44 Getty Images: Gavin Parsons / Oxford

Scientific (br). USDA Agricultural Research Service: Stephen Ausmus (bl). 45 Corbis: Nigel Cattlin, / Visuals Unlimited (tr). Dorling Kindersley: Lynette Schimming (tl). 47 Dorling Kindersley: Natural History Museum, London (t). 48 Alamy Images: Andrew Darrington (tl). Jean Yves Rasplus: (bl). 50 Corbis: Alex Wild / Visuals Unlimited (tl). 51 Shane Farrell: (crb). 52–53 naturepl.com: ARCO. 54 Science Photo Library: Steve Gschmeissner (r). 55 Corbis: Nigel Cattlin / Visuals Unlimited (tl). 56 Corbis: Lida Van Den Heuvel / Foto Natura / Minden Pictures (bl). FLPA: Pete Oxford / Minden Pictures (tl). 57 Corbis: Lida Van Den Heuvel / Foto Natura / Minden Pictures (b). 58 Corbis: Jef Meul / Foto Natura / Minden Pictures (bl). Dorling Kindersley: Natural History Museum, London (br). 59 Dorling Kindersley: Natural History Museum, London (tr). 60 Alamy Images: blickwinkel / Hartl (tl). Dorling Kindersley: Natural History Museum, London (br). www.kaefer-der-welt.de: (bl). 64 Corbis: Jef Meul / Foto Natura / Minden Pictures (tl). Dorling Kindersley: Natural History Museum, London (br). 65 Corbis: Alex Wild / Visuals Unlimited (br). 66–67 Dorling Kindersley: Thomas Marent (c). 67 Dorling Kindersley: Jerry Young (cr). 68–69 Corbis: Chris Mattison / Frank Lane Picture Library (bc). 70–71 Igor Siwanowicz. 74 Alamy Images: blickwinkel / Hecker (ba). Getty Images: Keith Porter / Oxford Scientific (tl). 75 Institute for Animal Health, Pirbright: (tl). 76 Bugwood.org: Joseph Berger (tl). FLPA: Dave Pressland (bl). 76–77 The Natural History Museum, London: (tc). 77 Corbis: Bert Pijs / Foto Natura / Minden Pictures (bl). Dorling Kindersley: Natural History Museum, London: (tr). 78 Corbis: Jan Van Der Knokke / Foto Natura / Minden Pictures (b). 80–81 Science Photo Library: Thomas Shahan. 82 Tom Murray: (b). 84 Dorling Kindersley: Natural History Museum, London (b). 85 Dorling Kindersley: Natural History Museum, London (cl). Dreamstime.com: Cathy Keifer (b). 86 Dorling Kindersley: Natural History Museum, London (t, bc, cr). 87 Dorling Kindersley: Natural History Museum (tc, bc). 88 Alamy Images: Andrew Darrington (tl). Dorling Kindersley: Natural History Museum, London (tc). 88–89 Dorling Kindersley: Natural History Museum, London (tc, bc). 89 Dorling Kindersley: Natural History Museum, London (cr). 90 Dorling Kindersley: Natural History Museum, London (bl). 91 Dorling Kindersley: Natural History Museum, London (tc, tr, bl). 92 Dorling Kindersley: Natural History Museum, London (tl, bc). 92–93 Dorling Kindersley: Natural History Museum, London (tc). 93 Dorling Kindersley: Natural History Museum, London (bl, br). 94 Dorling Kindersley: Natural History Museum, London (tl, bl). 95 Dorling Kindersley: Natural History Museum, London (c). 96–97 Igor Siwanowicz. 98 Dorling Kindersley: Booth Museum of Natural History, Brighton (br). 100 Alamy Images: B. Mete Uz (cl). 101 Dorling Kindersley: Natural History Museum, London (bc). 102 Alamy Images: Genevieve Vallee (tc).

Dorling Kindersley: Natural History Museum, London (br). 103 Corbis: Bert Pijs / Foto Natura / Minden Pictures (c). Photoshot: Imagebroker.net (b). 104 Dreamstime.com: Ryszard Laskowski (bc). naturepl.com: Premaphotos (clb). 105 Alamy Images: Michael Maconachie / Papilio (b). FLPA: Mark Moffett / Minden Pictures (tr). 106–107 Photoshot: A.N.T. Photo Library / NHPA. 108 FLPA: Piotr Naskrecki / Minden Pictures. 109 Corbis: Wayne Lynch / All Canada Photos (bc). 110 Photoshot: NHPA (bl). 111 Corbis: Dennis Kunkel Microscopy, Inc. / Visuals Unlimited (tl); Damon Wilder (cr); Wayne Lynch / All Canada Photos (br). 112 FLPA: Albert Lleal / Minden Pictures (tr). 113 Corbis: Stephen Dalton / Minden Pictures (tr). 114–115 naturepl.com: Ingo Arndt. 116 Ardea: David Spears (Last Refuge) (bl). 117 Dorling Kindersley: Photo Biopix.dk (cr). Getty Images: Kallista Images (tl). 118 Ardea: David Spears (Last Refuge) (tl). FLPA: Nigel Cattlin (tr). Getty Images: Elliot Neep / Oxford Scientific (bl). 119 Corbis: Science Picture Co / Science Faction. 120 Alamy Images: Premaphotos (tl). Corbis: Patrick Honan / Steve Parish Publishing (cl). Getty Images: Oxford Scientific (bc). 121 FLPA: D Jones (br). 125 Science Photo Library: Simon D. Pollard (br). 126–127 Dorling Kindersley: Thomas Marent. 128 Photoshot: James Carmichael Jr / NHPA (b). 129 FLPA: D Jones (bl). 130 FLPA: Thomas Marent / Minden Pictures (cl). 131 FLPA: Olivier Digoit / Imagebroker (bl). 132 Photoshot: David Maitland / NHPA. 133 Getty Images: Oxford Scientific (bc). 134 Corbis: Norbert Wu / Minden Pictures (c). 135 Corbis: Albert Mans / Foto Natura / Minden Pictures (br); Piotr Naskrecki / Minden Pictures (cl). 136 Alamy Images: Dave Bevan (c). FLPA: Photo Researchers (bl). 137 Getty Images: Don Farrall / Digital Vision (bl). 138 Dorling Kindersley: Staab Studios—modelmakers (l). 140–141 naturepl.com: Alex Hyde. 142 FLPA: Jan Van Arkel / Minden Pictures (b). 143 Corbis: Nigel Cattlin / Visuals Unlimited (cl). FLPA: Nigel Cattlin (crb). The Natural History Museum, London: (clb). Photoshot: N A Callow / NHPA (tr). 144–145 Dorling Kindersley: Jerry Young (b). 144 Alamy Images: blickwinkel / Hecker (tc). 145 Alamy Images: blickwinkel / Hecker (br). Corbis: Visuals Unlimited (tr).

Jacket images: Front: Dorling Kindersley: Booth Museum of Natural History, Brighton cr/ (bush hymenoptera); Natural History Museum, London fbr/ (giraffe weevil), fbl/ (violin beetle), fcla/ (shield bug), bl/ (assassin bug), fcra/ (blue night butterfly), fcr/ (blue pansy butterfly), fcla/ (tiger moth), cla/ (poecilocoris latus), cla/ (birdwing butterfly), cra/ (lacewing). Getty Images: Brand X Pictures / Brian Hagiwara c. Spine: Getty Images: Brand X Pictures / Brian Hagiwara tc.

All other images © Dorling Kindersley

For further information see:
www.dkimages.com